RECONSTRUCTION FOLLOWING THE CIVIL WAR IN AMERICAN HISTORY

Other titles *in American History*

IN
AMERICAN
HISTORY

RECONSTRUCTION FOLLOWING THE CIVIL WAR IN AMERICAN HISTORY

Marsha Ziff

Enslow Publishers, Inc.
40 Industrial Road   PO Box 38
Box 398   Aldershot
Berkeley Heights, NJ 07922 Hants GU12 6BP
USA   UK
http://www.enslow.com

Library of Congress Cataloging-in-Publication Data

Ziff, Marsha.
    Reconstruction following the Civil War in American history /
Marsha Ziff.
        p. cm. — (In American history)
    Includes bibliographical references and index.
    Summary: Traces the history of the Reconstruction period following
the Civil War, from 1865 to 1877, following the efforts of the Republican
party leadership to bring the South back into the Union and to give
former slaves their civil rights.
    ISBN 0-7660-1140-2
    1. Reconstruction—Juvenile literature. [1. Reconstruction. 2. United
States—History—1865–1898.] I. Title. II. Series.
E668.Z54 1999
973.8—dc21   98-46740
                                                       CIP
                                                        AC

Printed in the United States of America

10 9 8 7 6 5 4 3 2 1

To Our Readers:
All Internet addresses in this book were active and appropriate when we
went to press. Any comments or suggestions can be sent by e-mail to
Comments@enslow.com or to the address on the back cover.

Illustration Credits: Enslow Publishers, Inc., pp. 12, 100; Library of
Congress, pp. 8, 16, 42, 45, 62, 68, 76, 79, 80, 88, 105, 109, 110; The
Museum of the Confederacy, Richmond, Virginia, Copy Photography by
Katherine Wetzel, pp. 11, 22; National Archives, pp. 14, 19, 24, 26, 29,
35, 51, 72, 84, 95.

Cover Illustration: Library of Congress; National Archives.

★ CONTENTS ★

THE SOUTH IN RUINS

Twenty-five-year-old Robert Fitzgerald was shocked by the destruction that surrounded him as he traveled south to Virginia in 1866.[1] A teacher and former Union soldier, Fitzgerald had left behind his peaceful Pennsylvania home. On his journey he saw that the Southern landscape still bore the charred remains of houses and barns, although the Civil War had ended over a year earlier. Fitzgerald saw children, whose fathers had died in the war, pulling heavy plows alongside their widowed mothers. Gangs of hungry orphans scrounged through mounds of rotting garbage. No crops grew, and no farm animals grazed on the hillsides. Even the people appeared charred and ruined. Glassy-eyed, they moved like zombies. Everyone looked old and sad.

To his dismay, Fitzgerald observed farmers raking through fields where battles had been fought, turning up the skeletons of men and horses to use for fertilizer. Those soldiers who had survived the war resembled living skeletons. Many had lost arms or legs. Their ragged uniforms of the Confederate, or Southern, Army were held together with string because buttons with the insignia of the Confederate States of America were now forbidden.[2]

Cities throughout the South were devastated at the end of the Civil War. These children are sitting in the ruins of Charleston, South Carolina.

What brought Robert Fitzgerald to this wasteland of the South? He wanted to help. He knew that, besides rebuilding homes and replanting fields, there was other important work to be done. A black man himself, he had heard about the millions of freed slaves who longed desperately to learn. Previously oppressed by slavery, these "freedmen" now gazed at an unbounded future, but they lacked education. As slaves, they had been denied schooling. One former slave woman recalled: "If they [slave owners] caught us with a piece of paper in our pockets, they'd whip us. They was afraid we'd learn to read and write, but I never got the chance."[3]

Slowly, with the end of the war and slavery, the door to opportunity had begun to open, and Robert Fitzgerald was eager to help guide the former slaves through it. A serious scholar, he attended Lincoln University, a school for black men in Pennsylvania. When he heard General Oliver O. Howard, chief of the newly created Freedmen's Bureau, speak at the Lincoln University graduation exercises, he had been moved by the general's emotion. Howard had urged the students to have a share in the advancement of their race, and Fitzgerald had resolved to head south for the summer to do just that.

How well would Robert Fitzgerald and others like him succeed? The period of Reconstruction, which would last from 1865 to 1877, was a time of violence, confusion, and hope. An old order had died. What would take its place?

2

WAR!

In a Virginia woods in April 1865, Confederate General Robert E. Lee and his starving army were surrounded and out-numbered by Union troops. The Civil War that had begun with the firing of cannons on Fort Sumter in South Carolina was nearing its end. Lee knew he was defeated. Heartbroken, he sent a white flag— actually a white towel—with a note to Union General Ulysses S. Grant. On April 9, the two generals met at the house of Wilmer McLean in the town of Appomattox Court House, Virginia, to sign the articles of surrender. Then the two enemies shook hands, and Lee mounted his faithful horse, Traveller, and rode back to his con-quered troops. General Grant later remembered feeling "depressed at the downfall of a foe who had fought so long and valiantly and had suffered so much for a cause, though that cause was, I believe, one of the worst for which people ever fought."[1]

A "Glorious" Cause?

Although Grant echoed the sentiments of most Northerners, Southerners had felt differently. They fought fiercely for what they called "the glorious cause"—independence from the United States.[2] In

General Robert E. Lee, seen here on his horse, Traveller, surrendered his Confederate troops to Union General Ulysses S. Grant on April 9, 1865.

December 1860, South Carolina had seceded (withdrawn) from the United States. In February 1861, representatives from South Carolina and six other states proudly formed a new nation: the Confederate States of America. Over the next few months, other Southern states joined them. They chose Montgomery, Alabama, as their first capital and Jefferson Davis of Mississippi as their president. On May 21, the capital moved to Richmond, Virginia, only one hundred miles from the United States capital at Washington, D.C. The eleven states that ultimately made up the Confederacy were South Carolina,

Mississippi, Florida, Alabama, Georgia, Louisiana, Texas, Virginia, Arkansas, Tennessee, and North Carolina.

One of the issues that urged the Southern states to secede was slavery. Slaveholders in the South viewed owning slaves as a way of life. They also thought slaves were necessary to the Southern economy, which was based on cash crops grown on large plantations worked by slave labor. Abolitionists in the North believed slavery should be abolished, or done away with, and that all slaves should be emancipated, or set free. Though many Northerners were racially prejudiced and wanted only to

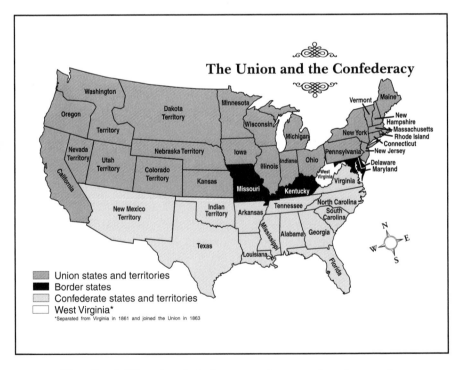

The Civil War divided the states between loyalty to the Union and the new Southern Confederacy.

end the influence of the slave states over the rest of the country, most in the North did believe slavery should end, somehow. Southerners came to fear that not only their economy but their entire way of life was in danger.

Slave Life

In the slaveholding South, the slave owner had power over the slave to buy, sell, punish, and even to kill. Slaves were considered property. In most states they could not legally marry, own land, or even be taught to read and write.

However, it was to the slave owner's advantage to provide for his slaves. Ample food, clothing, medical care, and material necessities were furnished so that the slaves would remain healthy. If they were well cared for, slaves could do more work and produce children who would grow to be strong, healthy slaves. A former slave remembered one Louisiana planter who liked to boast of the size and value of his young slaves. He said the planter often declared that raising slaves "'twas just like raisin' young mules."[3]

Nevertheless, many owners took a personal interest in their slaves, referring to them as their "people"— inferior members of their extended families who needed protection and guidance. Masters often spoke of their "love" for their slaves. This manner of caring for the slaves has been termed *paternalism*.[4] Slaveholders took a fatherly, or paternal, view of their slaves, who, they claimed, were content. An English visitor to the South in 1861 found many slaveholders eager to prove the happiness of their slaves:

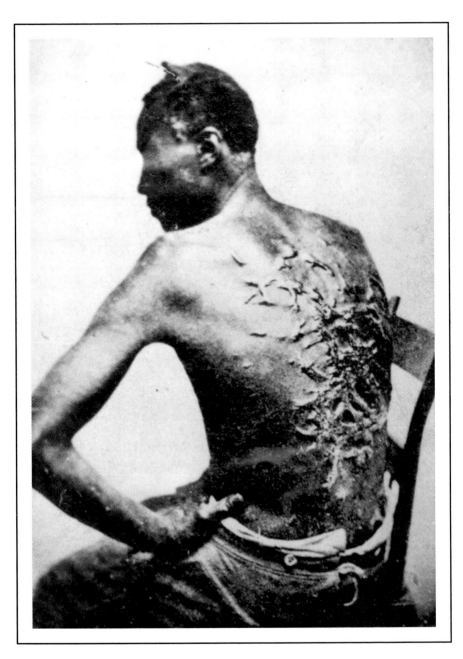

The slave master had complete legal control over his slaves and could give them any punishment he saw fit, including severe whippings that left the slave scarred for life.

"Are you happy?" a slave would be asked.

"Yas, Sar," the slave would quickly reply.

"Show how you're happy," demanded the master.

Rubbing his belly and grinning, the black man replied, "Yummy! Yummy! Plenty belly full!"

"That's what I call a real happy . . . chap," declared the white owner.[5]

Southern women also claimed a closeness with their slaves. A Florida woman went so far as to claim, "We never thought of them as slaves. They were 'ours,' 'our own dear black folks.'"[6]

But William Russell, an English visitor who traveled the South early in the war, was skeptical. If the slaves were content and passive, Russell wondered, why did plantation owners need to take strict measures to control their slaves, such as night patrols (which searched for runaway slaves) and curfews? "There is something suspicious," Russell concluded, "in the constant never-ending statement that 'we are not afraid of our slaves.'"[7]

Because slaves knew that they were viewed as possessions with no hope of advancement no matter how well they were treated, they often deliberately worked slowly, broke tools, and pretended not to understand orders. Their subtle resistance and lack of motivation revealed the hopelessness of their situation. In order to endure, they put up a front of ignorance. They learned to read their masters' moods and react accordingly. They shuffled their feet, scratched their heads, and grinned stupidly—putting on what they called "the darky act."[8]

And whenever they could, the slaves seized the opportunity to escape to freedom.

Although Southerners often pretended their slaves were happy, the slaves knew they were seen as property. They often engaged in work slowdowns as a subtle means of fighting back against the system of slavery.

The Underground Railroad

The Underground Railroad was "a [secret] network of paths through the woods and fields, river crossings, boats and ships, trains and wagons, all haunted by the specter [threatening possibility] of recapture."[9] Railroad "stations" were houses and churches; "agents" were people along the route who assisted the fugitive, or runaway, slaves.

The Fugitive Slave Law of 1850 appointed federal officers with the power to form posses to recapture runaway slaves anywhere in the United States. Thus the danger of being caught if a slave ran away increased, and the penalties for trying to escape were strengthened. Still, some courageous people continued to fight slavery by means of the Underground Railroad.

One of the boldest leaders, or "conductors," of the Underground Railroad was Harriet Tubman, herself a fugitive slave. In 1849, she had walked, following the North Star, from Bucktown, Maryland, to Pennsylvania, braving the dangers all fugitives faced—darkness, prowling bloodhounds, and roaming slave hunters on horseback. She returned to the South many times after her own successful escape to help others make their escape from slavery. Among those she helped were her own parents, whom she took to Canada, where slavery was illegal.

Division Between North and South

The system of slavery, which rejected the idea of working for wages, along with the slaves' resistance and lack of education, contributed to the slowness of Southern advancement. The free states of the North, on the other hand, moved ahead rapidly in manufacturing, financial wealth, and literacy.

Although not all Northerners were abolitionists, slavery had been dying out in the North since the early 1800s as the economy came to be based more on manufacturing and trade, rather than on farming alone. City life and factory work were not well suited to slavery. But even after the importation of slaves from Africa became illegal in 1808, slavery in the South flourished. The demand for cotton increased, and, by 1860, slavery had become the backbone of the Southern economy because plantation owners used slaves to work the cotton fields. Southerners called their system of slavery the "peculiar institution," not because it was odd, but because it was unique.[10]

Although only a minority of Southerners owned slaves, even those with small farms and no slaves looked down on blacks and favored slavery. Plantation owners sometimes lent their farm equipment to the small farmers and provided jobs for members of their families. Many farmers were hired as overseers, slave drivers, or to hunt down fugitive slaves. Those with ambition hoped to own slaves themselves one day. And many poor whites felt the only thing that kept them socially higher than blacks was the color of their skin. Thus, the majority of Southerners, slave owners or not, supported the peculiar institution and preferred Southern life just the way it was.[11]

States' Rights

The Southern states did not like the federal government telling them what to do. They perceived a strong federal government as a threat to their way of life, so they

When the Southern states seceded from the Union, they elected Jefferson Davis their president.

proclaimed states' rights, or the right of each individual state to form its own policies.

Advocates of states' rights believed that the United States Constitution was a compact of the states as "separate, independent sovereignties."[12] Because they saw the states as independent, they believed a state could break the agreement of the Constitution and leave the Union if it disagreed with the policies of the national government. But many advocates used the defense of "states' rights" as an excuse to preserve and continue slavery and spread it into new territories.

In the presidential election of 1860, the Democratic party supported slavery and states' rights, whereas the Republicans opposed slavery, or at least the spread of slavery, and favored a strong federal government. As soon as Republican Abraham Lincoln was elected, South Carolina began secession proceedings.

The Southerners, often called "Rebels," believed their states had the right to secede and form a new government, the Confederate States of America. Regarding this new government, Confederate Vice President Alexander H. Stephens stated:

> Our new government is founded . . . upon the great truth that the negro is not equal to the white man. . . . This . . . government, is the first in the history of the world based upon this great physical, philosophical, and moral truth.[13]

The Confederates were willing to fight for their independence just as the American colonies had fought against England in the Revolutionary War less than one hundred years earlier. So, on April 12, 1861, the American Civil War officially began when Confederate cannons fired on Northern-occupied Fort Sumter in the Charleston, South Carolina, harbor.

Throughout the war, Confederate soldiers expressed faith in their cause in letters home. On July 4, 1863, an Alabama corporal wrote a letter from the battlefield. In it, he declared he was convinced he was fighting for "the same principles which fired the hearts of our ancestors in the revolutionary struggle."[14] Another Southern officer wrote, "I am willing to fall [die] for the cause of Liberty and Independence."[15]

A Long Night of Tyranny

Many Northern soldiers believed as the South did—that *they* were fighting for the patriotic ideals of the American Revolution. The Northerners, or "Yankees," viewed the Confederates as traitors, and they, too, expressed their views in letters. One Connecticut soldier wrote that if "traitors be allowed to overthrow and break asunder ties most sacred . . . all the hope and confidence of the world in the capacity of self-government will be lost . . . and perhaps be followed by a long night of tyranny."[16]

An Ohio lieutenant received a letter from his ten-year-old son. The father wrote back, commenting that the boy's neatly written letter

> tells me that while I am absent from home, fighting the battels [sic] of our country, trying to restore law and order to our once peaceful & prosperous nation, and endeavoring to secure for each and every American citizen of every race the rights garenteed [sic] to us in the Declaration of Independence . . . I have children growing up that will be worthy of the rights that I trust will be left for them.[17]

Confederate soldiers, like Private Benjamin T. Long of the 40th North Carolina Troops, considered themselves revolutionaries like their ancestors who had fought in the American Revolution.

Praiseworthy Soldiers

"In case I should be shot please send this to my home."[18] So wrote Robert Fitzgerald inside the cover of his diary, when he was a private in the 5th Massachusetts Cavalry, before heading into battle at Petersburg, Virginia, in 1864.

Robert Fitzgerald was one of many black soldiers who fought for the Union in the Civil War. He had at first enlisted in the Navy, where after four months he had become ill with malaria. When his ship reached Massachusetts, he was sent to Chelsea Naval Hospital. On January 14, 1864, he was discharged from the Navy, and on January 15 he volunteered as a private in the 5th Massachusetts Cavalry, an all-black regiment.[19] Although his army career was also brief (he again became ill and was honorably discharged), his service brought his family a feeling of pride for generations.[20]

At first, the United States government had not wanted to allow black men, whether they had been slaves or not, to fight. But when the Union feared it might be losing the war, the War Department had organized the 1st South Carolina Volunteers on November 11, 1862. It was the first black regiment with official military status.

The 54th Massachusetts Volunteers

An all-black regiment that became famous was the 54th Massachusetts Volunteer Infantry Regiment. Its men fought valiantly to capture Fort Wagner in South Carolina on July 18, 1863. Although the attack failed and more than three hundred soldiers died, the 54th

In the later years of the Civil War, many black soldiers fought bravely for the Union cause.

Massachusetts displayed great courage. To those who had doubted that courage, *Atlantic Monthly* magazine said, "Through the cannon smoke of that dark night, the manhood of the colored race shines before many eyes that would not see."[21]

African-American soldiers were earning a reputation as fearless heroes. They even earned presidential praise. In a public letter on August 26, 1863, Abraham Lincoln addressed anyone who was against freeing the slaves or allowing them to enter the military. He wrote: "You say you will not fight to free negroes. Some of them seem willing to fight for you."[22]

A ROUGH START

Even before Abraham Lincoln became president, he was aware of the problems created by slavery. Although in every state people disagreed over the slavery issue, Lincoln had spoken out boldly at the Illinois Republican Party Convention in Springfield in June 1858, when he accepted the nomination for United States senator. Quoting the Bible, he said, "A house divided against itself cannot stand." He continued, "I believe this government cannot endure, permanently half *slave* and half *free*."[1] He knew that slavery and freedom were incompatible, and he feared the nation would become divided over the slavery issue.

Sadly, Lincoln's fears were realized. By the time he was inaugurated as president of the United States in March 1861, the new Confederate States of America had emerged. The following month, the Civil War began. Lincoln became passionately determined to see the country reunited. He made it his solemn vow to "preserve, protect, and defend" the United States government.[2] He worried that the Union would crumble and disappear.

Planning for Peace During Wartime

While the war raged, President Lincoln devised his plan for peace and unity. Among the questions he faced were:

Even before he became president in 1861, Abraham Lincoln feared that the issue of slavery would tear apart the nation.

On what terms should the defeated Confederacy be reunited with the Union? Who should establish these terms, Congress or the President? What system of labor should replace plantation slavery? What should be the place of blacks in the political and social life of the South and of the nation at large?[3]

The Emancipation Proclamation

As part of his plan to hasten the end of the war, Lincoln signed the Emancipation Proclamation on January 1, 1863, hoping to weaken the Southern rebellion by encouraging loyalty to the Union. The Emancipation Proclamation declared slaves to be free only in those states still rebelling against the Union. Commenting on this, *The London Spectator* newspaper remarked that the principle behind the Emancipation Proclamation "is not that a human being cannot justly own another, but that he cannot own him unless he is loyal to the United States."[4] Lincoln hoped that the proclamation would encourage some Confederate states to return to the Union if they believed they could keep their system of slavery, at least temporarily. Because it had the potential to weaken the Southern states and end the war, the Emancipation Proclamation played an important role in convincing England and France not to intervene in the war on the side of the Confederacy.

In reality, the federal government lacked the authority to enforce the law in the states of the Confederacy. Nevertheless, the Emancipation Proclamation made the abolition of slavery the primary focus of the war.

SOURCE DOCUMENT

. . . ON THE 1ST DAY OF JANUARY, A.D. 1863, ALL PERSONS HELD AS SLAVES WITHIN ANY STATE OR DESIGNATED PART OF A STATE THE PEOPLE WHEREOF SHALL THEN BE IN REBELLION AGAINST THE UNITED STATES SHALL BE THEN, THENCEFORWARD, AND FOREVER FREE; AND THE EXECUTIVE GOVERNMENT OF THE UNITED STATES, INCLUDING THE MILITARY AND NAVAL AUTHORITY THEREOF, WILL RECOGNIZE AND MAINTAIN THE FREEDOM OF SUCH PERSONS AND WILL DO NO ACT OR ACTS TO REPRESS SUCH PERSONS, OR ANY OF THEM, IN ANY EFFORTS THEY MAY MAKE FOR THEIR ACTUAL FREEDOM.[5]

On January 1, 1863, President Lincoln signed the Emancipation Proclamation, which freed the slaves in those states Lincoln said were rebelling against the United States.

Abolitionist and former slave Frederick Douglass, although aware of the limitations of the proclamation, said he saw it as "more than it purported, and saw in its spirit a life and power far beyond its letter. Its meaning to me was the entire abolition of slavery, wherever the evil could be reached by the federal arm, and I saw that its moral power would extend much further."[6]

In the South, many slaves saw the proclamation as an opportunity to flee north. Slaves who had previously escaped to the protection of the Union Army had been declared "contraband of war" by General Benjamin Butler in 1861, and for the rest of the war, they were known as contrabands. Butler used the Southerners' argument that slaves were property against them, by taking away their "property" as contraband, or illegal, goods in wartime. The former slaves lived in contraband camps, where abolitionists provided them with schools, jobs, and medical care. Now many more blacks crowded into the camps.

Northerners were impressed by the former slaves' eagerness to join the Union Army and by their passion to learn. Missionary teachers who taught at the contraband camps were inspired. One teacher reported from Norfolk, Virginia, in 1864, "The children . . . hurry to school as soon as their work is over. . . . Old men and women strain their dim sight with the book two and one-half feet distant from the eye, to catch the shape of the letter."[7]

Proclamation of Amnesty and Reconstruction

On December 8, 1863, nearly a year after signing the Emancipation Proclamation, Lincoln

Frederick Douglass, the famous former slave and abolitionist leader, rejoiced at news of the signing of the Emancipation Proclamation. Despite its limitations, it seemed to be a giant step toward Douglass's dream of abolition in America.

issued his Proclamation of Amnesty and Reconstruction. With this proclamation, the president offered to pardon the Southern states for their revolt. The proclamation promised the people of the South "full pardon and the restoration of all rights . . . to persons who resumed their allegiance [to the Union] by taking an oath of future loyalty, and pledged to accept the abolition of slavery."[8]

The proclamation granted that whenever the number of men who took the oath of loyalty to the Union in any Southern state amounted to 10 percent of that state's voters in the presidential election of 1860, the state could set up a government with representation in Washington, D.C. Then the Southern states could handle the race problem in their own way. Many Radical Republicans opposed the proclamation.

Who Were the Radicals?

Those Republicans who wanted to abolish slavery and create a better, fairer South were called Radicals because of their extreme views. These zealous men were committed to dramatic social change. Senator Benjamin Wade, himself a Radical, described them: "The radical men are the men of principle; they are the men who feel what they contend for."[9]

The number of Radicals increased as the war progressed. Some Radicals were passionate abolitionists who cried out for equal rights for blacks. Others were more concerned with seeing the Southern aristocracy, which had been based on the system of plantation slavery, come to an end. Radicals were found not only among government officials but also among ordinary citizens. While

Radicals differed on many issues, they agreed that the war provided the perfect opportunity to end slavery and remake the South.

As the war continued, more Radicals rallied around the cause of justice for blacks. Radical abolitionist Wendell Phillips remarked that Lincoln's 10 Percent Plan "frees the slave and ignores the negro."[10] Phillips believed Lincoln's plan did not tackle the problem of what to do with the millions of blacks once they were freed. Phillips and other Radicals feared the freed slaves would be abused by the Southern states.

The abolitionist paper *The Anti-Slavery Standard* claimed that "to commit the care and education of the freedmen to those revived [Southern] states is too much like giving the lambs to . . . the wolves."[11] Radicals believed the federal government had an obligation to protect all its citizens, including the freed slaves.

Struggles Over Policy

Because they viewed Lincoln's Proclamation of Amnesty and Reconstruction as too lenient, Congress proposed the Wade-Davis Bill in 1864. The Wade-Davis Bill required that Reconstruction be delayed until 51 percent, rather than just 10 percent, of voters in each Southern state had pledged to support the United States Constitution. Congress passed the bill on the last day of the congressional session, but Lincoln pocket-vetoed it. That is, he refused to sign it, so that, once Congress adjourned, the bill could not become law. The Radicals were furious, and a debate arose over whether the president or Congress should have the power to establish Reconstruction policy.

Congress took a radical step in January 1865, by proposing the Thirteenth Amendment to the United States Constitution. Because slavery still existed, especially in the slaveholding border states that had remained loyal to the Union, the Thirteenth Amendment called for the abolition of slavery throughout the nation. President Lincoln gave the amendment his support.

Then, in March, Congress created the Freedmen's Bureau to protect the interests of Southern blacks. The Freedmen's Bureau was a powerful agency designed by the Radical Republicans to restructure the South by providing medical services, schools, land, and better working conditions for the freedmen. Most of the bureau's officials were army officers. The bureau was unpopular among many white Southerners because it interfered with their state governments.

SOURCE DOCUMENT

SECTION 1. NEITHER SLAVERY NOR INVOLUNTARY SERVITUDE, EXCEPT AS PUNISHMENT FOR CRIME WHEREOF THE PARTY SHALL HAVE BEEN DULY CONVICTED, SHALL EXIST WITHIN THE UNITED STATES, OR ANY PLACE SUBJECT TO THEIR JURISDICTION.

SECTION 2. CONGRESS SHALL HAVE THE POWER TO ENFORCE THIS ARTICLE BY APPROPRIATE LEGISLATION.[12]

The Thirteenth Amendment to the Constitution, which would be ratified in December 1865, formally outlawed slavery in the United States.

Thus, even before the war was over, Congress and the president were already struggling with the problems presented by Southern Reconstruction.

Tragedy Strikes

It had taken four long, bloody years, but the Civil War finally ended after Confederate General Robert E. Lee surrendered to General Ulysses S. Grant on April 9, 1865. On April 14, President Lincoln and his wife, Mary Todd Lincoln, were enjoying a rare evening of entertainment and relaxation at a play entitled *Our American Cousin*.

The play was a comedy, and at one particularly hilarious part when everyone was laughing loudly, the audience was startled when a man, pistol in one hand and dagger in the other, leapt onto the stage from the presidential box. Was this part of the play? they wondered. Then the screams began: *The president has been shot!*

Above the din, it was believed the strange man cried, "*Sic semper tyrannis!*" ("Thus always to tyrants"—the motto of Virginia). Then he limped offstage as quickly as he was able. Crowds rushed to the presidential box. When Dr. Charles A. Leale arrived on the scene, he found President Lincoln paralyzed, his head bloody. It was later learned that the bullet had entered the back of Lincoln's head and lodged behind his right eye. Soldiers rushed to carry the unconscious president to a nearby boardinghouse.

Doctors attended their gravely wounded patient throughout the night but were unable to save him. At 7:22 the following morning, April 15, 1865, President Abraham Lincoln died.

The strange man who had jumped to the stage after shooting the president was an actor named John Wilkes Booth, a fanatical Confederate sympathizer. He and an accomplice were cornered and killed in a tobacco barn in Virginia by Union cavalry before the end of the month.

New President, New Plans

Within hours of Lincoln's assassination, Vice President Andrew Johnson was sworn in as president of the United States. The following month, he announced his own Reconstruction plan. This plan offered pardons to all white Southerners except wealthy Confederate supporters and those who had been Confederate leaders, who would be required to apply individually for presidential pardons. Johnson talked of punishing the Confederates as traitors. This pleased the Radical Republicans, who wanted the federal government to take a firm hand in making drastic changes in the South. The major change the Radicals called for was equality for blacks.

Charles Sumner

One of the most zealous advocates of equal rights was Radical Charles Sumner. Courageous and outspoken, the Massachusetts senator was the first major American politician to insist that the freed slaves be given the right to vote. In addition, he demanded land, homes, and a government-sponsored program of education and social welfare be provided as well.

Charles Sumner had already suffered for his fearlessness. On May 19, 1856, at a time when the debate over slavery was growing more violent, he had spoken out in the Senate against Senator Andrew Pickens Butler of South Carolina. Butler supported the proslavery government of Kansas, and Sumner was relentless in his criticism. On hearing Sumner's speech, Senator Butler's nephew, Congressman Preston Brooks, was enraged. On May 22, Brooks came to his uncle's defense. Appearing at Sumner's desk in the Senate, Brooks repeatedly whacked Sumner over the head with his cane. Sumner's speech, Brooks declared, was "a libel [a damaging, unjust statement] on South Carolina, and Mr. Butler, who is a relative of mine."[13]

Senator Sumner, trapped behind his bolted-down desk, was defenseless against the blows. He finally escaped his tormentor only by ripping the desk from the floor and staggering, semiconscious, down the aisle. "I wore out my cane," Brooks later told his brother.[14]

Charles Sumner, the famous Radical senator, had been brutally attacked for his views against slavery. During Reconstruction, he worked hard to help secure civil rights for the former slaves.

Shocked and badly injured, Charles Sumner did not fully recover for three years, during which time his Senate seat was kept vacant, awaiting his return.

And what happened to Preston Brooks? He became a hero in the South. Although he resigned from the House of Representatives, he was reelected, and he returned to Washington, D.C. While at home, he received a brand new cane with a gold head, to replace the one he had broken in the attack, from the mayor of Columbia, South Carolina. Another cane, presented to him by the city of Charleston, bore the inscription, "Hit Him Again."[15]

When Andrew Johnson became president, Charles Sumner met with him nearly every day. Because of his past career, Johnson had given the Radicals cause to believe he would support them. As a congressman and later as a senator, Johnson had spoken against the "pampered, bloated, corrupted [Southern] aristocracy" and declared himself on the side of the common man.[16] Sumner came away from the meetings thinking the president agreed that the freed slaves should receive the right to vote.[17] He was in for a surprise.

Congress versus the President

The Radicals in Congress soon learned that President Andrew Johnson wanted each Southern state to determine for *itself* what rights its freed slaves should have. Also, the president was determined that Reconstruction should be in his hands, not Congress's.

The blacks meant nothing to Johnson. "White men alone must manage the South," he remarked in 1865.[18] On February 7, 1866, Frederick Douglass headed a black delegation to urge the president to grant blacks the right to vote. Johnson claimed to be their friend, but he said that giving blacks the vote would lead to race war. He also told them it was up to the states to decide who should vote. In his opinion, the best thing would be for the former slaves to leave the country.[19]

When the Radical Republicans saw President Johnson's true colors, they were bitterly disappointed. They became determined to prevent Reconstruction from falling into the hands of the president and thus the individual Southern states. They knew that no state, North or South, had ever given blacks increased political rights before. Why should they start now?

Violent disagreements erupted between the president and Congress over Reconstruction policy. At the heart of these disputes were the slaves. The South had been losing its grip on slavery as the war progressed. Once the war was over, the Thirteenth Amendment to the Constitution was ratified, in December 1865. By this action, the government declared all slaves in the United States officially free. But would freedom fulfill all the hopes, expectations, and dreams of the former slaves and their children?

4

FREE AT LAST?

Nearly 4 million black people rejoiced to see the answer to their prayers. At last they were their own masters!

What did freedom mean for individuals who had been enslaved all their lives? It meant they now owned their own bodies. Houston H. Holloway, a former slave who had been sold three times before he turned twenty, later expressed how he had felt when slavery ended. He said, "I felt like a bird out of a cage. Amen. Amen. Amen. I could hardly ask to feel any better than I did that day."[1]

In addition, freedom meant the ex-slaves could bundle up their few belongings and walk away from those who had held them in bondage. It meant they could go wherever they chose, whenever they chose. And many did. Eager for independence, throngs of freed people left the plantations where they had lived and labored.

A former slave remembered: "Right off colored folks started on the move. They seemed to want to get closer to freedom, so they'd know what it was—like it was a place or a city."[2] And many did indeed head for towns and cities, where they sought out black schools and churches, the protection of the army and the Freedmen's Bureau, and jobs. They hoped to find work that paid well and provided them with independence. Applying skills they had learned on the plantations, many became carpenters, blacksmiths, mechanics, waiters, seamstresses, porters, or laundresses. Although few got rich, those who found good jobs gained priceless personal satisfaction. The majority did not leave the South, and between 1865 and 1870, the black population of the ten largest cities in the South doubled.[3]

The freedmen were so eager to travel that railroads had to run extra trains. The ability to come and go as they pleased was a constant source of excitement.

For many, freedom also meant an endless search for family members who had been sold years before. Most slave owners had thought nothing of splitting up families if circumstances required, and to the slaves, this was the most terrible thing of all. So devastating was it, in fact, that nearly seventy-five years after the end of slavery, former slave Anna Harris said she would never let a white person into her house. Why not? Because when she and her sister Kate were slaves, they had been separated. Kate had been sold, and Anna had not seen or heard from her again.[4]

Once freed, many former slaves spent the rest of their lives seeking loved ones and struggling to return to the location where they had been parted. A reporter from the North wrote about his experiences in Virginia and North Carolina after the war. There, he saw "men . . . who had come from distant . . . States, seeking work or looking for relatives. One man . . . had walked from Georgia in the hope of finding at Salisbury [North Carolina] a wife from whom he had been separated years before by sale."[5]

Sadly, for those freed people whose destinations were towns or cities, disappointment often awaited. Decent homes were scarce. Frequently, the good jobs were already taken by city dwellers, and ex-slaves had to settle for menial, low-paying work. They lived in their own shantytowns on the outskirts of Southern cities. Poverty, filth, and disease reigned. Consequently, the rush to the cities dwindled after 1870.[6]

Those who stayed on the plantations displayed a new attitude. They demanded (but seldom received) high wages for their labor. More common was the "agreement" a Mississippi planter had with his ex-slaves. He told them, "you shall do the work; we'll make a crop of cotton, and you shall have half. I'll provide for ye . . . and when ye won't work, [I'll] pole [beat] ye like I always have."[7]

But many ex-slaves refused to grow cotton because they associated it with their slavery days. According to Frances Butler Leigh, who tried to revive her family's plantation after the war, the freed blacks were troublesome. They now refused to remove their hats when speaking to whites, worked only when they wanted, and carried guns.

White people were terrified. Many former Confederates fled to Mexico, South America, Canada, or Europe. A few, unable to face the failure of their society, committed suicide. But most tried to endure at home. Longing for the "good old days" when masters were masters and slaves were slaves, many white Southerners, particularly women, began to create in their imaginations tales of a glorious time with loyal, simpleminded slaves.

This myth of the "Lost Cause" affected all aspects of life, including art, literature, and entertainment. It continues to this day.

Eager to Learn

By the time teacher Robert Fitzgerald arrived in Virginia in 1866, thousands of blacks roamed destitute. Freedom had not brought them the instant happiness they had dreamed of, but rather, a lack of shelter, jobs, and food. They had found out, in the words of former slave Felix Haywood, "that freedom could make folks proud but it didn't make 'em rich."[8] However, although the freed people were without material possessions, they clung to hope and a strong desire for knowledge. They believed education could make them truly free.

So eager were the freed people to learn that Fitzgerald was nearly overwhelmed by the workload at Big Oak School in Amelia Court House, Virginia. He did not return to Pennsylvania at the end of the summer as planned but stayed in Virginia for over a year, teaching people of all ages. His enrollment increased from eight to 160. He taught six hours a day, five days a week, and two nights a week for two hours, for those who worked all day. He was thrilled to see his students advance in spite of the efforts of some to keep them oppressed.[9] Unfortunately, the war was not over in the minds of many white people, who still expected obedience from a race they believed to have very few rights at all.

The Freedmen's Bureau

To assist the freedmen in attaining their rights, the Bureau of Refugees, Freedmen, and Abandoned Lands, or the Freedmen's Bureau, was established by Congress in March 1865. Among its purposes was the distribution of food, clothing, and fuel to homeless freedmen. The bureau would provide the freedmen with land and schools as well. It also provided supplies for Southern whites who had lost or been forced from their homes during the war. Although the bureau would be given

The Freedmen's Bureau, established by Congress in May 1865, just after the end of the war, was designed to help the former slaves as they made their transition to freedom and self-sufficiency. Ideally, as depicted in this drawing, the bureau would stand between the former slaves and the hostile Southern whites who had held them in bondage for so many years.

much power and responsibility, it was intended to last only one year—long enough to help the freed slaves get on their feet. During that year, the bureau was authorized to divide abandoned and confiscated Southern land into forty-acre plots for rental and eventual sale to freedmen. The bureau also built hospitals and provided medical care for the freed slaves.

In February 1866, Congress authorized the continuation of the Freedmen's Bureau, but President Johnson vetoed the authorization. However, in July 1866, Congress overrode the president's veto and passed a new Freedmen's Bureau Bill, which extended the life of the bureau. The bureau would continue until 1869. During its existence, the Freedmen's Bureau built more than four thousand schools for black children. Most black colleges, including Fisk and the Hampton Institute, were founded with its aid.

"Forty Acres and a Mule"

Even before the creation of the Freedmen's Bureau, Union General William Tecumseh Sherman had initiated a land distribution program. When his army had marched through and devastated Georgia and South Carolina near the end of the war, thousands of slaves had escaped the plantations and followed his troops. Now homeless, they begged General Sherman for land. On January 16, 1865, he had issued his Special Field Order No. 15, which set aside islands and coastland from South Carolina to Florida for blacks only. Each freed family would receive forty acres of land, clothing, farm equipment, and seed. General Sherman also suggested that the army lend the people mules. Thus the dream of possessing "forty acres and a mule" was born in the hearts of the freedmen.[10] Many ran to buy halters for their promised mules and colorful pegs to mark off their promised land.

To the freed slaves, owning land was freedom. With his own land to cultivate, the freedman could become a self-sufficient member of American society. Unable to attain land himself, the freedman looked to the government to provide. By June 1865, the Freedmen's Bureau had settled nearly ten thousand families on land that had been abandoned by or confiscated from plantation owners. The freedmen believed this land was theirs to keep. But soon President Johnson insisted on returning the land to its original owners. What prompted him?

On May 29, 1865, President Andrew Johnson had issued his Proclamation of Amnesty, which included pardons for Southerners who pledged loyalty to the Union and promised to support emancipation. With the pardon was included restoration of all property except slaves. Once they were pardoned, the former Confederates regained their land.

By the end of 1866, nearly all the land the Freedmen's Bureau had provided for the former slaves had been taken away, and the former slaves' hopes were crushed. In line with his Proclamation of Amnesty, President Johnson also officially canceled Sherman's Special Field Order No. 15. Johnson demanded that the land Sherman had provided the blacks be returned to its original owners. In reality, General Sherman had arranged for the strip of coastal land and islands between Charleston, South Carolina, and Jacksonville, Florida, to be provided to homeless blacks only temporarily. However, the freedmen had believed their Union liberators were giving them a start on the road to freedom by providing them with land.[11] Now, deprived of what they thought was theirs, blacks were forced to go to work for white landowners who, in many cases, were their former masters. A bit of freedom slipped from their fingers.

A New Relationship

Once the land was restored to its original owners, confusion arose because of the new relationship between former masters and former slaves. They were now employers and employees. Many white landowners wanted to return to the way things were during slavery,

During the early years of Reconstruction, the issue of land ownership was one that made the slaves question the value of their new-found freedom. Hoping to get away from the big plantations that had held them in slavery, some freedmen settled together in freedmen's villages, like this one in Arlington, Virginia.

when blacks had worked in closely supervised groups. The only difference now was that, because slavery had been abolished, the blacks would receive either payment in cash or a share of the crop, as well as housing and food. This share-wage method was unsatisfactory, however, because employers frequently did not fulfill their part of the bargain, and blacks were cheated. Because few blacks had been well educated during the years of slavery, it was easy for white landowners to deceive their black employees and refuse to give them the money or share of crop they deserved.

By 1867, sharecropping had become common. Under the sharecropping system, individual families of former slaves became responsible for a specific plot of land. The sharecroppers were entitled to receive one third of the year's crop if the landowner supplied the tools, fertilizer, animals, and seed, and one half of the crop if the sharecroppers provided their own equipment. Most blacks preferred the sharecropping method because it enabled them to work individually with little supervision.

Although the former slaves did not own the land and were often mistreated by the white landowners, blacks did have a say in their new working conditions and could negotiate the terms of contracts with their employers. This, however, often proved difficult for poorly educated former slaves who were often not literate enough to understand fully the contracts they signed. Blacks, therefore, remained dependent upon whites. More than seventy years after the slaves were freed, former slave Thomas Hall still resented that dependence. Hall said,

Lincoln got the praise for freeing us, but did he do it? He give [*sic*] us freedom without giving us any chance to live to ourselves and we still had to depend on the southern white man for work, food, and clothing . . . in a state of servitude but little better than slavery.[12]

The Fourteenth Amendment

In June 1866, Congress proposed the Fourteenth Amendment to the Constitution. The amendment officially granted citizenship to blacks. The Fourteenth Amendment was a drastic upheaval because nine years earlier a slave named Dred Scott, whose master had died while they were living in a free state, had sued for his freedom and lost. In the infamous *Dred Scott* decision of 1857, Supreme Court Chief Justice Roger B. Taney declared that no black person could be a United States citizen.

The Fourteenth Amendment overturned the *Dred Scott* decision. It decreed that *all* states must grant the freed slaves their rights as citizens. One of these was the right to vote. The amendment also guaranteed that all federal and state laws would apply to both whites and blacks, and it barred anyone who had supported the Confederacy from holding high political office.

President Andrew Johnson did not approve of the Fourteenth Amendment. All of the Southern states rejected the Fourteenth Amendment except Tennessee, which became the first state readmitted to the Union, even though it had not yet granted blacks the right to vote.

The Reconstruction Act

The Radical Republicans of Congress continued to oppose the president and to fight for the rights of the freedmen. Then, in March 1867, something astonishing happened to renew the freedmen's hope. The Radicals, who took charge of Reconstruction in 1866, passed the Reconstruction Act over President Johnson's veto. The act ordered the Southern states to grant suffrage (the right to vote) to the freedmen. The act also commanded each Southern state to ratify, or formally approve, the Fourteenth Amendment before its rights as a state of the Union could be restored.

The Reconstruction Act divided the Southern states (except Tennessee, which had already ratified the Fourteenth Amendment) into five military districts, each under the control of a military commander who would make sure all black males were permitted to register to vote.

Most Southern whites were not happy. A Freedmen's Bureau agent in Edgefield, South Carolina, reported on their reaction. He said, "As the blacks were not considered as having rights while they were slaves, there seems to be difficulty in having a recognition of the fact that they have them now."[13]

JOHNSON AND THE RADICALS

At the time Andrew Johnson became president, after Abraham Lincoln's assassination in 1865, he was on good terms with the Radical Republicans. The Radicals thought that Lincoln's policy for Reconstruction had been too easy on the South. They believed President Johnson's policy would be stricter. They had good reason to hope, because Johnson had continually referred to the Confederates as traitors and demanded that they be brought to justice. Many times the Radicals had heard him declare, "Treason must be made odious [hateful] and traitors punished."[1]

Johnson also approved of the end of slavery. The Radical newspaper *New Orleans Tribune* predicted that, as president, Johnson would confiscate (seize) land from rich Southern landowners and redistribute it to the freedmen. After one of numerous meetings between President Johnson and several of his colleagues, Radical Senator Benjamin Wade triumphantly declared, "Johnson, we have faith in you. By the gods, there will be no trouble now in running the government."[2]

No doubt Senator Wade was unaware that Andrew Johnson had announced early in his political career,

"Some day I will show the stuck-up aristocrats who is running the country."[3] Now, although the president and the Radicals agreed that the Southern aristocrats must be brought to justice, they would soon disagree fiercely over who was running the country.

Radicals and blacks became disillusioned when they realized they had badly misjudged Johnson's politics and racial views. He was not as strict with the South as they had expected, and he believed Reconstruction should be in *his* hands, not Congress's. Why had he mislead them? the Radicals wondered.[4] A split began to grow between the president and the Radical Republicans in Congress.

The Government in Conflict

Johnson's background may hold clues to his behavior. He was from a poor North Carolina family and had worked as a tailor in Tennessee before entering political life. He despised the rich Southern aristocrats and supported the Union during the Civil War. When he was a United States senator from Tennessee, Johnson chose to remain in the Senate even after Tennessee seceded. After Nashville fell, President Lincoln asked Johnson to give up his Senate seat to become military governor of Tennessee. Ever loyal to the Union, Johnson gladly accepted his new assignment.

Two years later, he accepted the vice-presidential nomination. In his campaign speeches, he cried out against the Confederates, to the delight of the Radical Republicans. Although Andrew Johnson was a Democrat, he had been chosen as vice-presidential candidate by a Republican president—Abraham Lincoln. By choosing Johnson, Lincoln wanted to appeal to as many people as possible. On November 8, 1864, Lincoln won re-election, and Andrew Johnson became vice president of the United States.

Johnson cared greatly about the welfare of the poor white people in the South. In fact, he was convinced the yeomen, or small farmers, had been forced into secession and war by the wealthy plantation owners. Johnson believed that once they had a strong Democratic leader to champion them (he had himself in mind), the yeomen would form solid state governments.[5] Although he believed in the Union, Johnson, as a Democrat, had always supported states' rights.

Because of his hatred for the rich slaveholders, Johnson approved of the end of slavery. Thus blacks were encouraged. Johnson had once told a group of blacks in Tennessee,

Andrew Johnson, who grew up in a poor North Carolina family, hated the aristocratic Southern planters.

"I will indeed be your Moses, and lead you through the Red Sea of war and bondage to a fairer future of liberty and peace."[6] However, it turned out that Johnson was not as much opposed to slavery as he was to the wealthy slave owners. "Damn the Negroes," he once remarked. "I am fighting those traitorous aristocrats, their masters."[7] The aristocrats, in return, hated Johnson.

Johnson's Amnesty Proclamations

On May 29, 1865, President Johnson had issued two proclamations outlining his Reconstruction plan. The first offered amnesty (pardon) to all rebels who took an oath of loyalty to the Union and promised to support emancipation (the freeing of the slaves). However, in the second proclamation, Johnson designated fourteen classes of Southerners who would be required to apply individually to him for their pardons. Included in these were major Confederate officials and landowners whose property was valued at more than twenty thousand dollars. Johnson's proclamations were designed to make things difficult for the rich landowners.

But soon his threats of punishing the rebels faded. The Southern aristocrats flocked to him, begging him to restore their states to the Union as quickly as possible. Johnson gave in to their pleas. By 1866, he had issued more than seven thousand individual pardons to Southerners who fell under the twenty-thousand-dollar clause in his Proclamation of Amnesty.

Why did Andrew Johnson give in to the wealthy Southern landowners so easily? No doubt there were many reasons, some political, others personal. For one thing, the aristocrats appealed to Johnson's vanity.[8] They flattered him and begged him to restore their land to them. He enjoyed the attention of people who had once looked down on him as "poor white trash."[9] Perhaps he felt like a "Southern gentleman" at last.[10]

The former Confederate leaders and rich Southern landowners had outsmarted the president. Although they received presidential pardons, many who were pardoned were not really sorry they had seceded from the Union. They merely desired a speedy return to the lifestyle they had enjoyed before the war. Johnson had unwittingly made this possible. He was now on their side and was opposed to the Radicals in Congress, who remained determined to punish the Confederates and make drastic changes in the South.

There was another possibility for Johnson's apparent change of attitude. Andrew Johnson had a reputation as a heavy drinker. He drank before being sworn in as vice president. His speech was so rambling and slurred that the press taunted him as a "drunken clown."[11] At the time, Johnson was recovering from typhoid fever and had eaten little for days. He hoped the whiskey would perk him up, but it had gone quickly to his head.[12] President Lincoln had defended him, saying Johnson had made a bad mistake but was no drunkard. Still, Johnson was humiliated. It has been suggested that his embarrassment in front of Congress led to feelings of alienation from the very people who might have been able to assist him in creating a successful Reconstruction policy—the Radical Republicans.[13]

The Fight Continues

President Andrew Johnson continued to argue with the Republicans in Congress over the problems of Reconstruction. The Democrats, who were in the minority, supported the president, who had also been a Democrat. Although the majority of congressional members were Republican, they disagreed among themselves as well. Conservative Republicans agreed with the president that the federal government should stay out of the South's affairs, but they did wish to protect the freedmen from violence. Moderate Republicans also wanted to protect Southern blacks. They agreed that Johnson's policy was too lenient but did not want to oppose the president.

Only the Radical Republicans spoke out boldly in favor of black equality. The Radicals opposed the president by arguing that civil rights must be guaranteed by the federal government. They believed that the freedmen were American citizens with all rights, including the right to vote.[14]

The Radicals insisted that black suffrage was necessary so that the blacks could protect themselves against persecution and unfair laws. To those who questioned how the freedmen could vote when they could not read or write, Radical Republican Carl Schurz responded that voting was the only way for blacks to secure an education. Schurz also explained that not all blacks were illiterate. He mentioned as an example the many blacks in Louisiana, who, according to Schurz, "are as highly educated, as intelligent, and as wealthy as any corresponding class of whites."[15]

"Restoration"

President Johnson preferred to call Reconstruction "restoration."[16] He maintained that the Southern states had never technically been out of the Union. He was ready to renew their representation in Congress. In each Southern state, the president appointed a provisional governor who, although a Southerner, had been loyal to the Union. Johnson was confident the states would do well in handling their "restoration" themselves.

Johnson did not require the Southern states to give the freedmen the right to vote, and Radicals feared a return to slavery. Congressman Thaddeus Stevens called the president's course "madness."[17] In light of the Radicals' hostility, the president feared they were dangerous, and even out to kill him. To calm them, he asked Mississippi Provisional Governor William L. Sharkey to include black suffrage in the new state constitution. But Johnson stipulated that the right should extend only to black men who could read and write and who owned property worth at least $250. Of course, this would narrow the number of freedmen who would be allowed to vote. Sharkey ignored Johnson's request altogether. The Radicals continued to intensify their opposition to the president, especially after the Southern states passed their "Black Codes" late in 1865.[18]

The Black Codes

The Black Codes passed by the Southern states greatly restricted the lives of the freedmen. Among other injustices, the codes required blacks to obtain special licenses to work and to sign annual contracts with their employers, whom the contracts referred to as "masters." As Radical Republican Benjamin J. Flanders had predicted, the Southern states were devoting "their whole thought and time . . . to plans for getting things back as near to slavery as possible."[19]

The harsh treatment of blacks forced many Northerners to side with the Radicals. The *Chicago Tribune* confronted Mississippi, which, along with South Carolina, had enacted the first and most severe of the Black Codes. The *Tribune* challenged,

> We tell the white men of Mississippi that the men of the North will convert the State of Mississippi into a frog pond before they will allow such laws [Black Codes] to disgrace one foot of the soil in which the bones of our soldiers sleep and over which the flag of freedom waves.[20]

"The Separation Complete"

In order to provide more protection to blacks, Congress had passed the Civil Rights Act early in 1866. The Civil Rights Act declared all persons born in the United States (except American Indians) to be citizens with equal rights regardless of race.

President Johnson vetoed the Civil Rights Act, as he had the Freedmen's Bureau Bill earlier. His vetoes only increased his bitter struggle with Congress. Moderate Republicans joined with the Radicals against him. On April 9, 1866, a united Congress repassed the Civil Rights Act over Johnson's veto. Afterward, regarding this final break between the president and Congress, a Republican newspaper headline announced, "The Separation Complete."[21] Congress then also repassed the

Freedmen's Bureau Bill over Johnson's veto. Congress was gaining control of Reconstruction.

Violence Erupts

Under their feeble Johnson-appointed governments, the Southern states went from bad to worse in their treatment of blacks. On a street in Memphis, Tennessee, on May 1, 1866, two horse-drawn taxis collided—one driven by a white man, one by a black. When police arrived and arrested the black driver, three days of racial violence ensued. White mobs assaulted blacks on the street and invaded South Memphis, where many families of black soldiers lived. At least forty-eight people were killed (all but two of whom were black), five black women were raped, and hundreds of black homes, churches, and schools were plundered or burned.

Twelve weeks later, in New Orleans, Provisional Governor James Madison Wells called a constitutional convention to establish a new Louisiana state government. On the day of the convention, a mob made up mostly of Confederate veterans attempted to break up the gathering. Fighting broke out in the streets. By the time federal troops arrived, thirty-four blacks and three white Radicals had been killed and more than one hundred people injured in what would become known as the St. Bartholomew's Day Massacre.[22] Cyrus Hamlin, a Union war veteran, wrote that the slaughter he saw that day surpassed anything he had seen on the battlefield.[23]

The riots in Memphis and New Orleans proved President Johnson's Reconstruction policy a failure. Not giving up, he decided to go on a whistle-stop tour, a "swing around the circle" by train, from Washington,

AND BECAUSE I STAND HERE NOW AS I DID WHEN THE REBELLION COMMENCED, I HAVE BEEN DENOUNCED AS A GREAT TRAITOR. MY COUNTRYMEN HERE TO-NIGHT, WHO HAS SUFFERED MORE THAN I? WHO HAS RUN GREATER RISK? WHO HAS BORNE MORE THAN I? BUT CONGRESS, FACTIOUS, DOMINEERING, TYRANNICAL CONGRESS HAS UNDERTAKEN TO POISON THE MINDS OF THE AMERICAN PEOPLE, AND CREATE A FEELING AGAINST ME IN CONSEQUENCE OF THE MANNER IN WHICH I HAVE DISTRIBUTED THE PUBLIC PATRONAGE.

WHILE THIS GANG—THIS COMMON GANG OF . . . BLOODSUCKERS, HAVE BEEN FATTENING THE COUNTRY FOR THE PAST FOUR OF FIVE YEARS—MEN NEVER GOING INTO THE FIELD, WHO GROWL AT BEING REMOVED FROM THEIR FAT OFFICES, THEY ARE GREAT PATRIOTS![24]

As the Radical Republicans in Congress saw President Johnson's Reconstruction policies, they realized he was not as committed to the rights of the freedmen as Congress was. In speeches like this one given in September 1866, Johnson began to show his hostility toward Congress.

D.C., to Chicago to St. Louis and back to Washington, to plead his cause.[25] The tour was a disaster.

At every stop he was rude. Radicals claimed he was drunk.[26] In Cleveland, a member of the crowd yelled, "Hang Jeff Davis [the former president of the Confederacy]!" Johnson shouted back, "Why not hang Thad Stevens and Wendell Phillips [prominent Radical Republicans]?"[27]

President Johnson had finally lost control of himself and the country. In the congressional election of 1866, the Republicans defeated the Democrats by well over a two-thirds majority. The president's Reconstruction plan had failed. Congress, under the leadership of Radical Republican Thaddeus Stevens, was now in control of Southern Reconstruction.

The road to black equality was paved and ready.

6

THE KU KLUX KLAN

As Congress worked for black equality, many Southerners fought to maintain white supremacy. Enraged when the former slaves gained the right to vote and hold political office, whites frequently resorted to violence to deprive blacks of their freedom. An event that took place in 1875 shows the extent to which Southern whites were prepared to go to keep the former slaves from becoming equal citizens.

Murder in Cold Blood

On a quiet Christmas evening, former Mississippi State Senator Charles Caldwell decided to take a stroll. His wife begged him not to go. Caldwell was a top officer in the Mississippi state militia, and he and his wife both knew it was dangerous for a black man of his position to be out at night alone. Yet Caldwell insisted.

While Caldwell walked the silent streets of Clinton, Mississippi, he met, seemingly by chance, his friend Buck Cabell. Cabell was white.

"You must take a drink with me," Cabell urged.[1]

Caldwell declined but Cabell insisted. He put his arm around Caldwell's shoulder and escorted him to Chilton's store and bar.

Inside the bar, Cabell maneuvered Caldwell to the window. As Cabell raised his drink in a toast, Caldwell heard not the cheerful ring of glass against glass, but a terrible crash as the window shattered and the deafening boom of rifles. Bullets ripped into his flesh. Collapsing, he glanced up at Cabell, who had jumped back against the bar. No doubt Caldwell was horrified when he realized that his so-called friend had lured him to his death.[2]

White Supremacist Terror

The assassination of Charles Caldwell was just one of thousands of cold-blooded murders of blacks that took place in the South during Reconstruction. White Southerners had formed many terrorist groups with names such as the Knights of the White Camellia, Society of the White Rose, the Pale Faces, and the Red Shirts. Most of these organizations were allied with the Democratic party. Perhaps the most notorious of these groups was the Ku Klux Klan.

Innocent Beginnings

The Ku Klux Klan began innocently enough in the summer of 1866, when six young men who had been Confederate soldiers formed a club for amusement. Life was dull after the excitement of wartime, and they were hungry for fellowship and action.

John C. Lester, James R. Crowe, John B. Kennedy, Calvin Jones, Richard R. Reed, and Frank O. McCord founded the Klan in the law office of Calvin Jones's father, Judge Thomas M. Jones, in the small Southern town of Pulaski, Tennessee.[3] They took the name "Ku Klux Klan" from a college fraternity, Kuklos Adelphon,

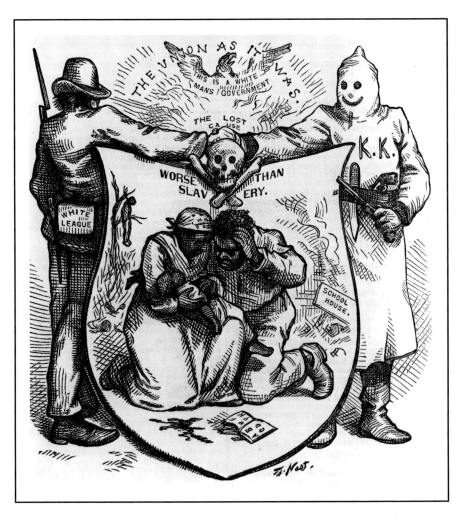

Political cartoonist Thomas Nast's depiction of the Ku Klux Klan joining with other white supremacist groups to keep Southern blacks from exercising their civil rights appeared in Harper's Weekly.

kuklos being the Greek word for circle or band. The unusual name attracted attention and may have contributed to the organization's rapid growth.[4]

The young friends invited new members and set up rules for their clique. Right from the start, everything about it was secret. Klan members disguised themselves in masks, flowing robes, and tall, pointed hats, some with horns protruding from the sides. The Klan adopted strange names and rituals. Its early officers were a "Grand Cyclops" or president, a "Grand Magi" or vice president, a "Grand Turk" or marshal, a "Grand Exchequer" or treasurer, and two "Lictors" or guardians of the meeting place. Later, in 1867, a more elaborate hierarchy of officers was created, with the office of Grand Wizard of the Empire at the top. Former Confederate General Nathan Bedford Forrest was elected as the first and only Grand Wizard.

The Klan's first meeting place, or "Den," was Judge Jones's office, but they soon moved to a dark, desolate grove outside of town. There, their elaborate initiation rites would be more mysterious and their chance of discovery slim.[5]

A Terrorist Gang

Although it began as a relatively harmless social club, within a year the Ku Klux Klan had snowballed into a terrorist gang, a "brotherhood" of white men sworn to victimizing and controlling blacks. What caused such a shocking transformation?

First of all, when the Civil War ended, the South was filled with confusion and lawlessness. Besides, Pulaski,

Tennessee, had always been a rough town, where shooting sprees and drunken scenes were common.[6]

Also, slavery was over. Radical Reconstruction was under way, and blacks were eager to enjoy equal rights. But there were whites who were not happy with this turn of events. The Ku Klux Klan became a tool dedicated to destroying, with violence, any accomplishments black people made during Reconstruction.

Wealthy whites who had owned large plantations and slaves before the Civil War expected blacks to continue to work for them. These aristocrats' entire way of life had been devastated by the war. One woman who had grown up on a plantation in Louisiana spoke of the genteel life to a Northern visitor after the war. She said, "No one had ever told us it was all wrong or that we were going on gaily toward an awful destruction."[7]

That "awful destruction" and the revolutionary changes it brought threw many whites into a panic. It frightened them that a people who had been slaves for nearly two hundred years could suddenly own land, hold office, and vote.

The Ku Klux Klan upheld white supremacy—the belief that the white race was created by God as supreme. The Klan declared that history proved white men had always ruled over "inferior" races. This was not a new idea. White supremacy had been alive and well throughout the United States for decades.

At secret initiation rites, men swore to uphold the Klan as their Christian duty. They vowed to break the law if necessary and to stick by one another, no matter what. The penalty for disloyalty was harsh indeed. Prospective Klan members were obliged to pledge:

1. We are on the side of justice, humanity and constitutional liberty, as bequeathed to us in its purity by our forefathers.

2. We oppose and reject the principles of the Radical party.

Any member divulging [telling], or causing to be divulged, any of the foregoing obligation, shall meet the fearful penalty and traitor's doom, which is Death! Death! Death![8]

Night Riders

In Greene County, Georgia, in 1869, Abram Colby's little daughter screamed as she watched a mob of Klansmen viciously beat her father for three hours. His crime? He had organized a large branch of Georgia's Equal Rights Association in 1866 and had been elected to the state legislature in 1868.[9] But throughout the South, all ex-slaves were targeted by the Ku Klux Klan, regardless of age, sex, or whether they held political office.

For example, a few miles north of Pulaski in Columbia, Tennessee, the Klan dragged a twenty-year-old black man from his home, strangled him, tied a rock to his neck, and dumped his body into the murky waters of the Duck River.[10]

Klansmen were often drunk on these nightly raids, and foul language flowed. Some carried whiskey bottles in their cone-shaped hats. Dressed in their costumes, with their horses also disguised, they claimed to be the ghosts of Confederate soldiers, hoping to scare blacks, whom they believed to be superstitious and gullible. Most blacks were not so easily fooled.

Victims of violence often recognized their attackers. An Alabama freedman who watched as his son was mutilated and killed knew one of the men who did it. "Dick Hinds had on a disguise," the freedman recalled. "Me and him was raised together."[11]

So whenever cloaked riders thundered up to a cabin at midnight, the occupants were terrified not because they believed the horsemen were departed spirits come to spook them, but because they knew their visitors were flesh-and-blood killers.

Robert Fitzgerald and the Ku Klux Klan

Robert Fitzgerald, who had come south in 1866 to help Reconstruction efforts as a teacher, had moved to North Carolina in 1868, married, and in 1869 had opened Woodside School near Chapel Hill. He was harassed by the Ku Klux Klan for his "Yankee" school. Late each night, he and his wife listened to the Klansmen galloping past their home, and in the morning they would find the ground around the schoolhouse trampled to bits.[12]

Fortunately, Klan activity against the Fitzgeralds did not go beyond these nightly disturbances, and Fitzgerald continued his teaching. Later, when seventy-five United States troops arrived in Chapel Hill, Klan activity quieted down.

Who Fought Back?

Did no one stand up to the Ku Klux Klan? Former North Carolina State Supreme Court Chief Justice Thomas Ruffin wrote to his son, who had joined the Klan, "It is wrong—all wrong, my son, and I beg you to have nothing to do with it."[13]

But Ruffin did not speak out publicly, nor did former North Carolina Governor William A. Graham, who was also opposed to the Klan. Graham was a popular man with much political influence, and people might have listened to him.

Sadly, Ruffin and Graham's silence was typical of many Southerners. No doubt they knew that men of power—planters, merchants, lawyers, local officials, even ministers—belonged to the Klan, and they were afraid.

The massive strength of the Klan dwarfed any efforts to fight it. In fact, the Klan was popular. Many women enjoyed sewing costumes for the night riders. Whites seemed to view violence against blacks as not really a crime, and the Klan continued to grow.

Why did the blacks not fight back? They, too, felt powerless against the aggressors. "The ku kluks klan is shooting our familys [*sic*] and beating them notoriously. We do not know what to do," one black man wrote to North Carolina Governor William W. Holden.[14]

The majority of freedmen sought to avoid retaliation. "We don't want to break the law or harm anybody. All we want is to live under the law," wrote one black man from a particularly violent area of Georgia.[15] But the law they desired to obey failed to protect them.

Furthermore, though many former slaves owned shotguns, these weapons were inferior to the Winchester rifles and six-shooters members of the Klan possessed. And although many blacks had served in the Union Army, they were outnumbered by whites who had been trained to bear arms since their youth.

"ONE VOTE LESS."—*Richmond Whig.*

This cartoon depicts a black man killed by the Ku Klux Klan in an effort to prevent him and other blacks from voting in the South during Reconstruction.

As a consequence, violence continued to increase, forcing governors in many states to declare martial law (military rule imposed on civilians during an emergency). Early in 1869, Governor William G. Brownlow declared martial law in Tennessee. This curtailed Klan activities for a short time. In Arkansas, Governor Powell Clayton placed ten counties under martial law and sent out a state militia composed of blacks and scalawags (Southern whites loyal to the Union) to arrest suspected Klan members. In 1870, Texas Governor Edmund J. Davis organized a special state police, 40 percent of whose members were black, to hunt down Klan members. The police made over six thousand arrests, successfully suppressing the Klan in that state.[16]

Eventually, in 1871, the federal government intervened. Congress passed three Enforcement Acts. These provided for troops and federal marshals to go south to attempt to protect black citizens. In April 1871, Congress passed the Ku Klux Act, which designated certain crimes, such as attempts to deprive citizens of their right to vote, hold office, serve on juries, or have equal protection under the law, as federal offenses. Under the Ku Klux Act, if the states did not punish the offenders, the federal government could do so. Democrats viewed this as a danger to states' rights. But by 1872, because the federal government took a strong hand in the Southern states against the Ku Klux Klan, Klan violence in the South began to fade.

In 1877, the federal government withdrew its troops from the South, giving terrorism free reign once again. Nevertheless, the Ku Klux Klan as an organization died out, only to reappear in 1915. At first, this new Klan was strong, but it, too, eventually faded out. The modern civil rights movement that began in the 1950s sparked a revival of the Klan.[17] Although the modern Ku Klux Klan, which still exists today, is not as strong as it was in the 1860s and 1870s, white supremacists continue to suppress, torment, and kill blacks, particularly in the South.

The Evil Continues

In the predawn hours of June 7, 1998, James Byrd, Jr., a black man, was murdered in the small town of Jasper, Texas.

First, Byrd was beat up. Then, he was chained to the back of an old pickup truck and dragged down a country road for nearly three miles. When the sun came up that day, pieces of Byrd's body were found scattered along the roadway.

Although the Ku Klux Klan and other white supremacist groups denied involvement in the lynching, a cigarette lighter with the Klan's insignia was found in the area. In addition, one young man who was convicted of murdering Byrd in February 1999 was a member of a white supremacist organization.

Thus, in spite of the efforts of the Radical Republicans in the 1860s and 1870s, racial prejudice still survives. However, during the years of Radical Reconstruction, many brave people, both black and white, worked diligently to assist blacks on the rough road to equality. Did they make any progress at all?

By 1867, the Radical Republicans had taken control of Reconstruction. The Reconstruction Act had divided the South into five military districts, with a United States Army general in command of each. To enforce the laws, two hundred thousand United States soldiers were stationed

THE RADICALS TAKE CHARGE

throughout the South. Under this military rule, blacks could safely register to vote. Army commanders were continually on guard at the polls to protect the former slaves from angry Southern whites.

Thaddeus Stevens

The powerful, courageous leader of the Radical Republicans was fiery old Thaddeus Stevens. Seventy-three years old when the Civil War ended, he had defended equal rights throughout his life. He believed the freed slaves should receive their own land as well as the right to vote.

Born with a club foot, the crippled Stevens empathized with those less fortunate. As a child, he had been teased by his schoolmates because of his limp. He knew how it felt to be different.

After Stevens was elected to Congress in 1848, he continued to speak out against slavery, calling it "a curse,

Until his death in 1868, Thaddeus Stevens led the efforts of the Radical Republicans in Congress to give the former slaves equal civil rights.

a shame, and a crime."[1] After the war, he led the Radical Republicans in their efforts to punish the rebels and gain equal rights for the freed slaves.

"The Great Obstruction"

President Andrew Johnson continued to oppose Thaddeus Stevens and the other radicals. He vetoed the Reconstruction Act and spoke out against rights for blacks. For the safety of the future of the Union, the Radical Republicans became determined to remove the president from office. Senator Carl Schurz said that many "saw in President Johnson a traitor bent upon turning over the national government to the rebels again."[2]

Because he made their efforts at Reconstruction so difficult, Johnson's enemies called him "The Great Obstruction."[3] On February 2, 1868, a resolution was made in the House of Representatives that Johnson "be impeached [accused] of high crimes and misdemeanors."[4] He would have to be accused and convicted of a specific crime in order to be removed from office.

Expressing the opinion of many, teacher Robert Fitzgerald, who had become active in politics in North Carolina, wrote in his diary on February 27: "Pres. Johnson impeached. Good!"[5]

Impeachment

Andrew Johnson's enemies wanted to remove him from the presidency. In order to do so, Johnson would have to be not only impeached, but also convicted by the Senate of having committed a specific crime. Thus the Radicals were hopeful when the House of Representatives sent the eleven articles of impeachment to the Senate and the trial was under way. But would the president be convicted of any actual crimes?

The impeachment trial of Andrew Johnson began March 30, 1868. Although Johnson's enemies cited many reasons for their accusation, the basic reason was that the president had hindered Republican efforts at Reconstruction. Johnson had vetoed twenty bills in three years and had removed Secretary of War Edwin Stanton from office, a move that violated the Tenure of Office Act. The Radical Republicans hoped to use Johnson's violation of the Tenure of Office Act as the specific crime of which to convict him, and remove him from the presidency.

According to the Tenure of Office Act, Johnson could not fire Stanton without the approval of the

Senate. Congress had passed the act to protect Stanton, who strongly supported Radical Reconstruction. The Republicans knew that Johnson wanted to remove Stanton, so by passing the Tenure of Office Act they had, in effect, set up the president.

At first, people were excited about the trial, the Senate chamber bursting with spectators and members of the House of Representatives. However, the trial dragged on for eight weeks, and people began to lose interest. Johnson presented a good defense, and although his accusers made a dramatic case against him, they were unable to find him guilty of any actual crimes.

Maine Senator William P. Fessenden said he would vote against the president if he "were impeached for general cussedness," but "that is not the question to be tried."[6] Thus, when the final votes were counted, they were one short of the two-thirds majority needed for conviction. President Andrew Johnson, unpopular as ever, remained in office.

Radicals in Power

In 1867, blacks in the South voted for the first time. The Union League, a political branch of the radical wing of the Republican party, encouraged them to vote Republican, as did the Freedmen's Bureau.

The majority of blacks did vote Republican. Black delegates were elected in each state to attend conventions to draw up new state constitutions. These progressive constitutions established in the South the right of all men to vote regardless of color, as well as a system of public education for all. They provided care for the poor and disabled and eliminated imprisonment for debt.

By 1868, seven Confederate states—Alabama, Arkansas, Florida, Georgia, Louisiana, North Carolina, and South Carolina—had ratified constitutions, installed Republican governments, ratified the Fourteenth Amendment, and been readmitted to the Union. By 1870, Virginia, Mississippi, and Texas were also readmitted. The states were united once again. Nevertheless, federal troops would continue to occupy the former Confederate states until 1877, to protect blacks and allow them to exercise their newfound rights.

Black Power

By 1868, blacks held positions of political power. For the first time, black policemen, lawyers, mayors, and judges were seen in Southern cities. Blacks and whites served together in government and sent their children to integrated schools. The new state governments set up public schools so everyone—black or white, rich or poor— could get an education. The part the Reconstructionists played in establishing a public school system for all children was perhaps their greatest achievement.[7]

But many whites opposed school integration. In Louisiana, when the children of black Governor Pinckney Benton Stewart Pinchback went to school, a police escort was there to protect them from hostile mobs.

A number of whites in Louisiana who were against integrated schools founded their own private schools. But both black and white pupils attended the public schools, and, according to the school superintendent, they got along fine.[8]

Blacks were elected to positions in the federal government as well as state governments. In 1870, Joseph H.

Rainey of South Carolina was elected to the House of Representatives, and Hiram Revels of Mississippi to the Senate. Among the highly educated blacks who served in Congress were James Rapier of South Carolina and Richard H. Gleaves of North Carolina. However, many black congressmen were self-taught. These included Robert Smalls of South Carolina, John Roy Lynch of Mississippi, and Jefferson Long of Georgia.[9]

During the early years of Reconstruction, while federal troops still occupied the South and the Freedmen's Bureau helped protect the rights of former slaves, many blacks rose to positions of political power, as depicted in this poster.

Black men also held state offices. Louisiana not only had its black governor, Pinchback, but also black sheriffs, policemen, and at least one black mayor: Monroe Baker, of St. Martin.[10] Henry McNeal Turner was a Radical leader in the Georgia legislature. J. W. Hood was a political leader in North Carolina. Mifflin Gibbs was municipal judge in Little Rock, Arkansas, and his brother Jonathan Gibbs held two state cabinet posts in Florida.[11]

Like most, Jonathan Gibbs had enemies. He was dedicated to the establishment of a strong system of public education in Florida. When his brother Mifflin visited him in Tallahassee, Mifflin found Jonathan living in a nice home, but with an attic bedroom filled with weapons. Jonathan told his brother that the Ku Klux Klan had threatened to kill him. And he did die suddenly, after a political banquet—the victim, many believed, of poisoning.[12]

The black men who obtained political power came from a variety of backgrounds. Pinckney Pinchback was the son of a white Mississippi planter and slave mother. Some black Reconstructionists were native Southerners. Some were "black carpetbaggers" (people who had come from the North to assist in Reconstruction). Some, like Pinchback, were of mixed blood; others were pure black.[13]

A number of black Reconstructionists entered politics through their work in the Freedmen's Bureau. Like Robert Fitzgerald, they came south to teach in schools sponsored by the bureau.

A large group of leaders were ministers. Jonathan Gibbs was a Presbyterian minister. Richard H. "Daddy" Cain, Henry McNeal Turner, and James D. Lynch were ministers of the powerful African Methodist Episcopal Church.[14]

Although the Reconstruction governments accomplished much good, Southern Democrats still did not like the fact that blacks could vote and hold office. According to historian W.E.B. DuBois, the one thing white Southerners "feared more than negro dishonesty, ignorance, and incompetency . . . was negro honesty, knowledge, and efficiency."[15]

The slow progress would too soon come to a halt, and a "Reign of Terror" would begin.

Carpetbaggers and Scalawags

Democrats in the South opposed the blacks' rise to power. They despised the men and women, both black and white, who came down from the North to help. These they referred to as "carpetbaggers," because it was said they carried all their earthly belongings in cheap suitcases made of carpeting.[16]

Southerners believed the carpetbaggers came to get rich. But the truth is they came for many reasons. Although some did view the South as a "happy hunting ground" where they could achieve political power and financial gain, others came to help economically or to assist in educating the freed slaves.[17] Most carpetbaggers were well educated, and not poor, as Southerners would have liked to believe. Their ranks included lawyers, teachers, Freedmen's Bureau agents, and businessmen. Carpetbaggers got involved in Republican politics. They supported the establishment of public school systems and civil rights legislation.

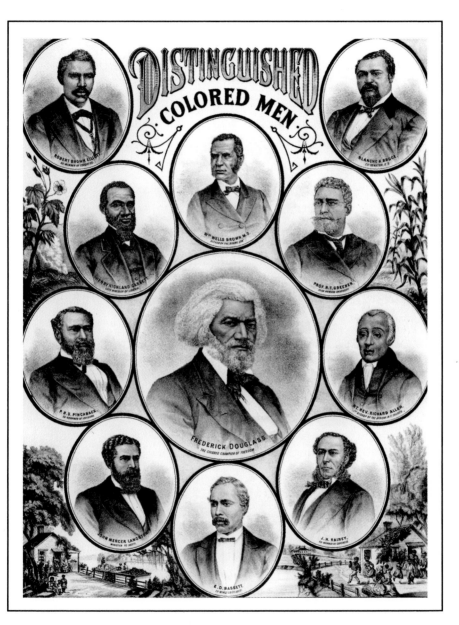

During Reconstruction, blacks became leaders not only in politics, but also in society, as ministers, teachers, merchants, and other professionals.

More numerous than the carpetbaggers were the "scalawags"—Southern-born whites who supported the Radical Republicans. The term *scalawag* evidently came from Scalloway, the tiny Scottish island known for its scrubby horses and cattle.[18] Scalawags were hated even more than carpetbaggers. They were referred to as traitors, lepers, and "white Negroes."[19]

Scalawags, like carpetbaggers, came from all walks of life. Even many Confederate veterans supported the Radical Republicans. One of the best known was General James Longstreet, who had fought alongside Confederate

Southerners hated the so-called carpetbaggers, those who came from the North to help Southern Reconstruction efforts. This cartoon was drawn by Thomas Nast.

General Robert E. Lee. Longstreet urged the defeated South to submit to Radical Reconstruction. In a letter to the *New Orleans Times* in March 1867, he wrote, "We are a conquered people" with "but one course left for wise men to pursue, and that is to accept the terms that are now offered by the conquerors."[20]

In 1868, Longstreet supported former Union general and Republican Ulysses Grant for president, and in

SOURCE DOCUMENT

I FELL INTO SOME TALK WITH [A MAN FROM CHARLESTON] CONCERNING THE POLITICAL SITUATION, AND FOUND HIM OF BITTER SPIRIT TOWARD WHAT HE WAS PLEASED TO DENOMINATE "THE INFERNAL RADICALS." WHEN I ASKED HIM WHAT SHOULD BE DONE, HE ANSWERED: "YOU NORTHERN PEOPLE ARE MAKING A GREAT MISTAKE, IN YOUR TREATMENT OF THE SOUTH. WE ARE THOROUGHLY WHIPPED; WE GIVE UP SLAVERY FOREVER; AND NOW WE WANT YOU TO QUIT REPROACHING US. LET US BACK INTO THE UNION, AND THEN COME DOWN HERE AND HELP US BUILD UP THE COUNTRY."

THE CITY IS UNDER THOROUGH MILITARY RULE; BUT THE IRON HAND RESTS VERY LIGHTLY. SOLDIERS DO POLICE DUTY, AND THERE IS SOME NINE-O'CLOCK REGULATION; BUT, SO FAR AS I CAN LEARN, ANYBODY GOES ANYWHERE AT ALL HOURS OF THE NIGHT WITHOUT MOLESTATION. "THERE NEVER WAS SUCH GOOD ORDER HERE BEFORE," SAID AN OLD COLORED MAN TO ME.[21]

The South resented the efforts of the North to rebuild Southern society in its own image. In this account, a New England reporter described his experiences in the South during Reconstruction.

1869 President Grant nominated Longstreet for the position of surveyor of customs for the port of New Orleans. The United States Senate confirmed his appointment.

Many white Southerners viewed Longstreet as a traitor for accepting a job from the Republicans. His former friend Harvey Hill wrote a letter to a local newspaper that said, "Our scalawag [Longstreet] is the local leper of the community."[22]

False Security

By 1870, many Republicans believed their party had attained its goals for Southern Reconstruction and that the worst was over. But opponents lurked, ready to spring at just the right moment and undo all the progress that had been made.

P.B.S. Pinchback sensed the danger as early as 1867. He warned, "There is a sense of security displayed by our people that is really alarming. They seem to think that . . . the Great Battle has been fought and the victory won."[23]

But, in reality, the battle was only beginning.

In 1868, while trouble brewed in many Southern states, hopeful freedmen voted in a national election for the first time. In Hillsboro, North Carolina, Robert Fitzgerald recorded that blacks "are casting their votes for the presidential candidates U.S. Grant [for president] and Schuyler Colfax [for vice president]. The citizens of Hillsboro are jubilant and their votes are going in like snowflakes, silently and surely. Everything is quiet and there seems to be the best feeling all around."[1]

THE SOUTH IN CRISIS

Sure enough, Grant and Colfax won, their victory decided by the votes of the freedmen. On November 6, the Republicans of Hillsboro celebrated with a grand parade.[2]

Ulysses S. Grant—Great General, Poor Politician

Unlike Andrew Johnson, Ulysses S. Grant was popular. He had been a great general and had led the Union Army to victory. Mainly because of his popularity, the Republican party had nominated him unanimously as their presidential candidate, even though he had not actively sought the nomination. Grant won the election

Triumphant Union General Ulysses S. Grant was elected president of the United States on the Republican ticket in 1868.

of 1868, defeating Horatio Seymour, the Democratic party's candidate. (President Johnson had not even been nominated.) Now, as president of the United States, the former general had just one request—"Let us have peace."[3]

And peace was needed. White supremacists in the South had formed terrorist organizations such as the Ku Klux Klan. During the 1868 presidential campaign, the Klan and similar organizations had used violence in many states to intimidate both black and white Republicans to keep them from voting. In Louisiana, more than one thousand people, mostly blacks, had been murdered between April and November.[4]

However, although Grant had succeeded as a general, he was not an effective president. He had no experience as a politician and was unsure how to bring about the peace he desired. During his first term, he was criticized for giving government jobs to relatives and friends, as well as for associating with rich men who expected his support in exchange for gifts and favors. His popularity also suffered because he was sometimes rude and ill-mannered with cultured men who made suggestions for government improvements.

By 1871, the term *Grantism* had come to represent corruption in government, bad taste in culture, and dishonesty in business—all the things reformers thought were wrong with America under Grant's administration.[5] But it would be unfair to say that Grant was responsible for all the problems. He was an honest man who sincerely wanted the best for the country. His worst crime was his inexperience.[6]

As Grant continued to plead for peace, white supremacist Democrats increased their Reign of Terror in many Southern states. For example, in Memphis, Tennessee, former Confederate General Nathan Bedford Forrest, as the Ku Klux Klan's Grand Wizard, warned, "There is not a radical leader in this town but is a marked man, and if trouble should break out, none of them would be left alive."[7] Ironically, with a former general as its president, the nation seemed to be on the brink of another Civil War.

The Fifteenth Amendment

During Grant's presidency, the Democrats gradually regained control of the Southern states. The majority of people in the North were tired of hearing about the old problems raised by Reconstruction. Current problems, such as high taxes and unemployment, concerned them more. Most Northerners were eager to see an end to the "everlasting Negro question."[8]

Radicals in Congress foresaw this situation and feared the Southern states would eventually deny blacks their right to vote. Not only that, but, surprising as it may seem, by the end of 1868, blacks could still not vote in eleven of the twenty-one Northern states. Consequently, Congress believed that a constitutional amendment guaranteeing blacks the right to vote in every state was essential.

As a result, the Fifteenth Amendment became part of the United States Constitution on February 3, 1870, after much hard work by Congress. Three versions of the amendment had been considered and debated. The first forbade all states to deny citizens the right to vote on grounds of race, color, or whether or not they had been slaves. The second version would, in addition, forbid the states to deny people the right to vote on grounds of

SOURCE DOCUMENT

SECTION 1. THE RIGHT OF CITIZENS OF THE UNITED STATES TO VOTE SHALL NOT BE DENIED OR ABRIDGED BY THE UNITED STATES OR BY ANY STATE ON ACCOUNT OF RACE, COLOR, OR PREVIOUS CONDITION OF SERVITUDE.

SECTION 2. THE CONGRESS SHALL HAVE POWER TO ENFORCE THIS ARTICLE BY APPROPRIATE LEGISLATION.[9]

In an effort to protect the voting rights of the former slaves in areas of the South, the Fifteenth Amendment was ratified on February 3, 1870.

literacy, property, or where they were born. The third, and most radical, declared that all male citizens twenty-one years old or older had the right to vote.

The first, most conservative, version was the one that passed, to the disappointment of most Radical Republicans. They knew that the first version had loopholes. A generation later, many Southern states would continue to take advantage of these loopholes to deny blacks the right to vote.

In the meantime, people continued to be distracted from Southern problems by current events.

Railroads and Westward Expansion

One of the things that took attention away from the South was westward expansion. The West held promise, and a large network of railroads opened the way.

May 10, 1869, marked the completion of the first transcontinental railroad. The Central Pacific Railroad had laid tracks eastward from Sacramento, California, and the Union Pacific had laid tracks westward from Omaha, Nebraska. When the massive project was finished, engines of both railroads touched noses at Promontory Point, Utah. The nation celebrated.

The railroads and western expansion provided jobs for many, and the economy boomed. Not only did men work on the railroads, but many families headed west by train, as well as covered wagon, to settle new land. Farmers and factories could produce more goods and ship them more quickly by train. Cattlemen went west to raise more cattle. Now they could ship their herds to market by train.

On May 10, 1869, the first transcontinental railroad was completed, opening the West to even further expansion.

Industry and the Golden Age of Invention

Industry was on the rise. When locomotives switched from wood to coal, coal mines multiplied. The huge steel industry was created when railroad tracks began to be made of steel rather than iron. And when railroads developed refrigerated freight cars to carry meat, the meat-packing industry was born.

Factories mass-produced shoes and clothing. Machines were invented that transformed society. By the end of 1866, sewing machines and washing machines were in popular demand. In 1868, Christopher Sholes received a patent for the first commercial typewriter. In 1874, John A. Peer's gear-cutting device enhanced the workings of locomotives and other machinery.

With the boom of Northern economy and industry, businessmen in the North viewed the South as a fertile ground for sales and investments. But they were hesitant to deal with the South because of the region's unstable political and economic condition.

In 1875, William E. Dodge, a New York capitalist, addressed the problem by declaring, "What the South now needs is capital [money] to develop her resources, but this she cannot obtain till confidence in her state governments can be restored, and this will never be done by federal bayonets."[10]

"Robber Barons"

Although the increase in business and industry was beneficial for many, individual men soon gained excessive wealth and power by buying up railroads and factories. These men would become known as robber barons because they wanted to set up their own financial empires and eliminate businesses that competed with them. They also used their power and money to influence government leaders.

The robber barons were extremely wealthy: John D. Rockefeller, who invested in oil and began the Standard Oil Company, was worth more than $815 million at the height of his career.[11]

In contrast, as the rich got richer, the majority of workers came to live in poverty. Factory wages did not keep pace with the cost of living, and working conditions became deplorable. Many women worked for more than twelve hours without sitting down or being permitted to use the bathroom. Immigrants competed with freed slaves for jobs, and slums sprang up on the fringes of the swanky neighborhoods where the robber barons lived. The poor workers came to hate the rich factory owners. One worker compared the situation to "the former feeling of bitterness between the North and South."[12]

Grant Faces Southern Terrorism

Busy dealing with both the benefits and problems of the rapid industrial and economic progress in the North, the federal government and the Northern states continued to ignore the increasing violence in the South. Amos Ackerman, President Grant's attorney general, wrote: "The Northern mind being active, and full of what is called progress, runs away from the past. Even such atrocities [wicked things] as Ku-Kluxery do not hold their attention."[13]

By 1870, due to the rise of terrorism, blacks and black sympathizers in the South were becoming too frightened to vote. They were engulfed in a wave of violence. Although the Fifteenth Amendment guaranteeing black suffrage had been ratified, Republican leaders in Congress saw that more was needed. To encourage blacks not to give up, Congress passed laws making interference with voters a federal crime. But how could the laws be enforced when people were afraid to speak up in their own defense? As a result, white supremacist Democrats began to replace Republicans in office.

When Governor William W. Holden of North Carolina feared he would be removed from office, he appealed to President Grant. Grant did not reply. When Democrats won the legislative election of 1870 in North Carolina, they impeached Governor Holden for "subverting personal liberty" in the state because Holden had overridden the North Carolina legislature and declared martial law to deal with the growing violence against blacks and their supporters. President Grant did not come to Holden's aid because he feared that tampering with the volatile situation could provoke another Civil War.[14]

But in 1871, when North Carolina and South Carolina teemed with chaos and destruction, Grant finally had to act. The state governments had failed to control the Ku Klux Klan, so Grant sent detectives to the South to uncover evidence and identify Klan members. Congress conducted an extensive investigation into the Klan. The federal government then arrested and prosecuted Klan criminals. Many were imprisoned for murder and other violent crimes. To escape punishment, some Klan members fled to Canada. Others surrendered, confessed, and were released or given lighter punishment.[15] By 1872, the Klan was stripped of its strength.[16] But the Southern Democrats still continued to regain power. The Republican Reconstruction governments in the South were on shaky ground.

The Campaign of 1872

Politics had changed drastically by the presidential campaign of 1872. Radical Republicans were losing their grip, the robber barons wielded power and influence, and a new group of reformers, the Liberal Republicans, had emerged. The Liberal Republicans claimed to want to undo the corruption that had crept into the government in recent years. They did not want Grant, whose administration was filled with scandal, to be reelected.

The Crédit Mobilier Scandal

One of the many scandals that plagued Grant's administration was the Crédit Mobilier affair. Crédit Mobilier was a corporation created by top officers of the Union Pacific railroad to build more railroads. The United States government lent money to Union Pacific to help pay for construction. When Union Pacific submitted bills to the government for expenses incurred by Crédit Mobilier, the charges were higher than the actual costs. The Union Pacific stockholders thus made a tidy profit.

Massachusetts Congressman Oakes Ames, who was a director of both Union Pacific and Crédit Mobilier, sold Crédit Mobilier stock shares at a low price to other politicians to keep them quiet.[17] When the *New York Sun* exposed the scandal on September 4, 1872, two members of Congress were expelled, Oakes Ames was censured, and the reputation of several other high government officials, including Vice President Schuyler Colfax, was damaged. (President Grant himself was not involved in the scandal.)

"Bayonet Rule"

As well as opposing government corruption, the Liberal Republicans were against Grant's use of military force, which they referred to as "bayonet rule," to calm the brutality in the South.[18] Federal troops still occupied the South and, in 1871, Grant had dispatched more troops to the most violent areas of the South in an attempt to quell the Ku Klux Klan.

Former Radical Carl Schurz had introduced Liberal Republicanism in 1871 in a speech in Nashville, Tennessee. Opposed to bayonet rule, he called for a return to "local self-government" for the Southern states.[19] The Liberals looked to the Democratic party for help in defeating Grant and attaining their goals. Their attitude did nothing to stop the rise of white supremacy and the approaching death of Reconstruction in the South.

The Surprise Candidate

Despite the problems of his administration, Grant himself remained popular. It was not going to be easy for the Liberals to defeat him. But fortunately for the Liberals, the Democrats also wanted to defeat Grant, and the two parties joined forces. Who would these unlikely allies pick to run against the president?

The Liberals first suggested Union General William Tecumseh Sherman. Sherman flatly refused, bellowing, "What do you think I am, a damned fool? Look at Grant! Look at Grant! What wouldn't he give now if he had never meddled in politics!"[20]

Then, at the Liberal Party Convention in Cincinnati, Ohio, in May 1872, a problem arose. The delegates could not decide between two candidates: Charles Francis Adams and David Davis. They compromised, and their choice shocked many. They nominated newspaper editor Horace Greeley.

Since before the Civil War, Horace Greeley had spoken out boldly and influenced public opinion in his powerful newspaper, the *New York Tribune*. He had opposed slavery and secession. Now he was a leading spokesman for reconciliation and local self-government in the South. So why did the nomination of this man, whose name was practically a household word, come as such a disappointing surprise?

"Anything to Beat Grant"

The Democratic party also nominated Greeley. However, the campaign slogan, "Anything to Beat Grant," made it obvious that neither Democrats nor Liberal Republicans considered Greeley their candidate of choice.[21] Although he was well known, he was not highly respected. In fact, because he rarely took a stand and stuck to it, Greeley had alienated many people. Another journalist, editor Henry Watterson of the *Louisiana Courier-Journal,* called Greeley "a queer old man, a very medley of contradictions, shrewd and simple, credulous and penetrating."[22]

The sixty-one-year-old Greeley was viewed by many as eccentric. Pudgy and childlike in appearance, he was a cartoonist's delight. Over the years, Greeley had supported such fads as vegetarianism and spiritualism. He had spoken out as strongly for war as for peace. Just as he himself seemed never to have had a clear direction, his campaign was marked with indecisiveness and confusion. Not surprisingly, on November 5, Grant won 56 percent of the popular vote—the highest percentage won by any presidential candidate between 1828 and 1904.[23]

By the time the election was over, Horace Greeley was exhausted. Devastated by his crushing defeat and grieving over the recent death of his wife, he died three weeks later. With him died the Liberal Republican party. But the issues it had raised remained alive.

Horace Greeley, editor of the New York Tribune, *was nominated for the presidential election of 1872 by both the Democrats and the Liberal Republicans.*

The Panic of 1873

In September 1873, the nation's economy unexpectedly collapsed. First, the gigantic banking firm of Jay Cooke and Company failed because it could not pay its debts. Then, many other banks shut down, forcing railroads, to whom the banks owed money, out of business. With no railroads to buy steel, 40 percent of the country's steel furnaces closed. Even the New York Stock Exchange closed down for a time.

The financial disaster caused panic among those who lost fortunes. More tragic, though, was the effect on workers. Now unemployed, they could not afford to house or feed their families. Several families were often crammed into one tiny apartment. They ate their meals at soup kitchens provided by charitable organizations. Crime increased.[24]

Overwhelmed by their own problems, Northerners felt more strongly than ever that the Southern states should deal with the "black question" themselves.

Sympathy for the South

Poverty increased in the South as well as in the North. Many people believed that the Reconstruction governments were responsible for the problems in the South. Some said allowing blacks to vote and hold office had been a big mistake. Northerners now felt sorry for the loyal Southerners and no longer feared they would start another Civil War. When Radical Senator Carl Schurz abandoned Reconstruction, white Southerners knew their time had come.

9

LEGACY

The Reign of Terror led by white supremacists nearly destroyed the dream of a free, integrated South. Although the Ku Klux Klan had been suppressed, other groups, such as the Red Shirts and Knights of the White Camellia, continued to spread terror throughout the South. By 1876, only in South Carolina, Louisiana, and Florida did black and white Republicans still hold political office, and they were able to do so only because voters were protected by federal troops. In the other Southern states, white Democrats ruled. They boasted of being the "white man's party." The Democrats wanted all federal troops out of the South. They were sick of "Yankee rule" and "Negro domination," and wanted what they called "home rule" or "Redemption."[1] Would the presidential election of 1876 grant the Democrats their wish by bringing an end to Radical Republican Reconstruction?

The Strange Election of 1876

President Grant was not nominated for a third term in 1876. Democrats and Republicans wanted reform, or improvement, in government. Republicans, most of whom now foresaw the end of Reconstruction, nominated Rutherford B. Hayes, the governor of Ohio, for president.

Hayes had been a general in the Union Army, and he had a degree from Harvard Law School. He was considered a respectable man who would prosecute corrupt government officials. This appealed to the reformers. A liberal, he believed the Southern states had the right to govern themselves. Although he showed concern for the freedmen, he was convinced the Southern states would protect blacks without bayonet rule. Hayes pledged to bring "the blessings of honest and capable local self government" to the South.[2]

The Democrats nominated New York Governor Samuel J. Tilden. Tilden had exposed and overthrown much corruption in the New York government. He called the Reconstruction governments a failure. He and the Democrats believed a Democratic victory was essential to weaken the power of the corrupt federal government and return power to the states.

Southern white supremacists, known as Redeemers, went into action to make sure Tilden was elected. They stepped up the violence.

In Mississippi during 1876, white supremacists drew the figurative "white line." This meant that whites were forced either to vote for Tilden, the Democrat, or face economic ruin or even death. They were so harassed that the majority of white Republicans in Mississippi either became Democrats or left the South.

In Louisiana, a Democratic leader said, "We shall carry the next election if we have to ride saddle-deep in blood to do it."[3] Republicans who refused to vote Democratic were fired from their jobs. Their names were printed in newspapers in what were known as "blacklists"; they were hunted down, whipped, and murdered.

Throughout the South, Democrats intimidated Republicans to keep them from voting or to force them to vote Democratic. Some Democrats also voted more than once themselves. Thus, in November 1876, Democratic presidential candidate Samuel Tilden apparently won the election. Or did he?

Who Won?

Tilden had 184 electoral votes, but needed 185 to be elected. Thus his supporters believed he would win easily. But a dispute arose between Democrats and Republicans over 20 electoral votes. Hayes had 165 votes. If he could gain the 20 disputed votes, he would win the election by one vote. Republicans accused Democrats of cheating. Democrats declared "Tilden or War!" and threatened to seize the White House.[4] Of course, neither candidate wanted another war. So Democrats and Republicans negotiated.

Congress formed a commission to study the complex issue. Finally, on March 2, 1877, the Democrats conceded the victory to Hayes; it was agreed he had won by an electoral vote of 185 to 184. Hayes, in turn, began to withdraw federal troops from the South. Republicans also agreed to provide federal funds to complete the Southern railroad system.

This "Compromise of 1877" marked the end of Reconstruction.[5] As black Louisianan Henry Adams declared, now "the whole South—every state in the South, had got into the hands of the very men that held us as slaves."[6]

For the time being, the Redeemers had won.

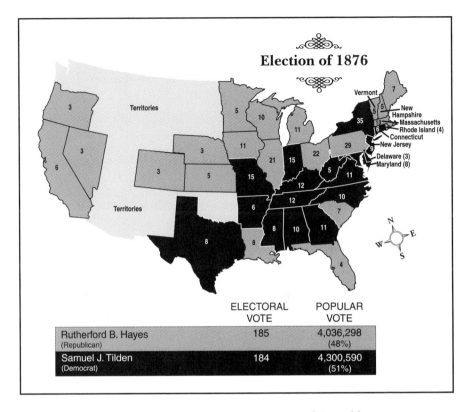

Election of 1876

	ELECTORAL VOTE	POPULAR VOTE
Rutherford B. Hayes (Republican)	185	4,036,298 (48%)
Samuel J. Tilden (Democrat)	184	4,300,590 (51%)

A compromise between the Democrats and Republicans in Congress gave twenty contested electoral votes to Republican Rutherford Hayes, electing him president in 1876.

The South Redeemed

"Redeem" means to recover ownership by paying a sum. By 1878, with federal troops gone, the Redeemers had recovered ownership of the South. The sum they paid for this ownership cannot be measured in dollars. Perhaps it can be measured in blood. They themselves had sworn to ride through blood to win, and their thousands of victims attest to the truth of their claim. They worked hard to suppress a race that was just beginning to emerge from bondage and to taste freedom in order to buy back their

Old South, instead of creating a new, better South where all people could enjoy freedom and equality.

The "Lost Cause"

Once the South was redeemed, whites launched an all-out race war against blacks. New laws and rules were designed to put blacks "in their place."[7] To the whites, that place was slavery. After 1878, the Redeemers labored to create a myth called the "Lost Cause." The Lost Cause was what Southerners had fought for and lost—the continuation of slavery and the plantation aristocracy.

Although they could not legally re-create actual slavery, Southern whites *could* create fanciful tales of the slavery days. These legends of the glorious days of the Old South told of a harmony between blacks and whites that never really existed.

Stories that depicted blacks as unable to care for themselves or their families also became fashionable. One told of a ten-year-old black boy who was kidnapped by his "wicked" black stepmother. The terrified boy begged to be returned to the kind white family that had cared for him.[8]

Another author wrote: "Poor little children nowadays, . . . can never know or understand the deep lasting love which existed between [white] Southern children and their [black] mammies."[9]

The South used such stories, and a system of laws called "Jim Crow," to keep the myth of the Lost Cause alive.

Jim Crow

The term *Jim Crow* was coined early in the nineteenth century to designate black people. It originated with a white entertainer, Thomas "Daddy" Rice, who imitated a black man by coloring his face and doing a song and dance called "Jump Jim Crow."[10] By the 1840s, the term was being used by abolitionist newspapers to describe the segregated railroad cars in the North.

But Jim Crow took on its most powerful meaning in the 1890s, after Southern whites had again taken control of their governments and were working to prevent blacks from exercising the rights they had won after the Civil War. Whites, intimidated by a new generation of blacks who had never been slaves, constructed an elaborate system of rules and laws to separate blacks from whites in nearly all walks of life. This system of segregation, which would last for many years, was called "Jim Crow."

On streetcars and trains, blacks were forced to sit in the rear. Signs were posted above the car doors as reminders, such as the sign in an Atlanta, Georgia, streetcar that read:

WHITE PEOPLE WILL SEAT FROM FRONT OF CAR TOWARD THE BACK AND COLORED PEOPLE FROM REAR TOWARD FRONT.[11]

In railroad stations, signs declaring "For White Passengers" and "For Colored Passengers" hung above separate entrances, ticket offices, and waiting rooms. Postings of "White Only" and "Colored" were common sights throughout the South—on park entrances, rest rooms, and water fountains.

In many areas, blacks were excluded altogether from recreational facilities such as amusement parks, bowling alleys, and swimming pools. Signs like "Negroes and Dogs Not Allowed" left no doubt about who was welcome in certain places.

In some states, blacks could patronize restaurants; small rooms and separate entrances were provided for them. In other states, blacks were barred completely from restaurants and lunch rooms.

Movie theaters had separate ticket booths, entrances, and seating. The seating for blacks was usually in the balcony. Refreshments were not available. Timothy Tyrone Taylor, five years old in Kernersville, North Carolina, as late as 1965, remembered sitting in the balcony with his older brother, munching chicken wings they had brought from home and tossing the bones into the darkness below.[12]

Schools

Just as most aspects of daily life were separated by race, black children in the South did not go to school with white children. During Reconstruction, some public schools were integrated, but that integration did not last long. Blacks generally attended their own schools. Black schools during Reconstruction were inferior because of the lack of financial support. The buildings were small, dark, and run-down. The children sat on backless log benches. The schools lacked basic supplies such as pencils, chalkboards, and schoolbooks.[13]

School conditions certainly did not improve under the Jim Crow system. In 1896, in *Plessy* v. *Ferguson*, the United States Supreme Court upheld a Louisiana law that required "separate but equal" accommodations on streetcars.[14] In the ruling, the Court rejected the appeal of Homer Plessy, who claimed that the Louisiana law violated his rights under the Thirteenth and Fourteenth amendments.[15] The "separate but equal" law, the essence of the Jim Crow period, came to apply to schools as well as to other public accommodations. But although they were separate, the schools were far from equal.

Robert Fitzgerald's granddaughter Pauli Murray attended a black grammar school in North Carolina in the 1920s. On her way to school each day she had to pass the white school—a beautiful brick building surrounded by a lawn filled with flowers. She was enchanted by the splendid playground, but she could only gaze through the tall fence topped with barbed wire before trudging off to her dilapidated wooden schoolhouse near the dump. Her school had no new books, no swings or slides, no working toilets or water fountains.[16]

Unfair as it may seem, blacks were expected to know and accept their place in the Jim Crow system. When whites felt that a black person had gone against the system, showing "sassy," or impudent, behavior, they punished him or her severely.[17] Taking the law into their own hands, the whites often resorted to lynching.

Lynchings

The word *lynch* means to kill someone, often by hanging, generally as a punishment for an alleged crime, without first going through the legal system.

After 1885, lynching became a common occurrence in the South. Blacks who were not submissive enough, in the opinion of some whites, were hanged, burned, or murdered in other ways. William J. Northen, a former governor of Georgia, was shocked when he realized that hundreds of white Southerners viewed blacks as animals deserving of death.[18] Actually, the whites themselves behaved like animals. Not only did they increase the violence against blacks, but in the late nineteenth and early twentieth centuries, they turned lynchings into public entertainment.

Newspapers announced the time and place for a lynching. People took off from work, and children were excused from school to attend. Later, the newspapers would report on the agony and death of the lynching victim under such headlines as "Colored Man Roasted Alive."[19]

People who attended snapped photos. Professional photographers made and sold postcards showing the

In the years after the end of Reconstruction, the South once again took drastic measures to keep blacks from attaining equality. Lynchings, like the one seen here, were common and often attracted enormous crowds of white Southerners.

corpses. Such cards were very popular, as were fingers and ears, which were sometimes chopped off and distributed as mementos while the victim suffered.[20]

Women as well as men were lynched. Mary Turner vowed to see the arrest and punishment of those who had lynched her husband. In response to her threat, a mob of several hundred whites, determined to "teach her a lesson," hung her upside-down from a tree and set her on fire.[21]

Of what crime was Mary Turner guilty? She had made "unwise remarks"; the whites did not like her attitude.[22] For similar "crimes," more than twenty-five hundred black men, women, and children were lynched in the South between 1885 and 1903. Bishop Warren A. Candler of Atlanta spoke out. "Lynching is due to race hatred and not to any horror over any particular crime, [and] unless it is checked it may involve anarchy," he argued.[23] But the murders continued. After many more years and gradually changing attitudes toward race relations, as well as better laws, lynching did end. However, the 1998 murder of James Byrd, Jr., in Jasper, Texas, shows that racial violence has not yet been stopped completely.

Modern Myth

Despite the overwhelming evidence of racial prejudice and cruelty, the myth of the Lost Cause begun by white Southerners during and after Reconstruction continues to this day. Racist memorabilia such as ornaments, postcards, candles, and dolls portray blacks as cheerful, simpleminded slaves. Although these items are referred to as "collectibles," they perpetuate a false image and glorify a tragic time in American history.[24]

Perhaps one of the best known stories exalting the myth of the Lost Cause is Margaret Mitchell's *Gone With the Wind*. Its loyal, trustworthy "Mammy" has come to symbolize female servants of plantation days.[25] Although the story is a good one, it is only that—a story. The reality was much more complex. And the fact remains that slavery has always been a terrible thing, which should never be glorified.

Reconstruction—Success or Failure?

All things considered, Reconstruction may appear to have failed. Many people never accepted the fact that slavery was a terrible thing. And yet, although their time was short and not all of their goals were realized, the Reconstructionists broke new ground and planted seeds of hope that continue to bear good fruit.

Brown v. Board of Education

The United States Supreme Court's *Brown* v. *Board of Education* decision of May 17, 1954, finally rejected *Plessy* v. *Ferguson*'s "separate but equal" doctrine. The *Brown* decision declared that segregation deprived "children of the minority group of equal educational opportunities," and thus, of the "equal protection of the laws guaranteed by the Fourteenth Amendment."[26]

No longer would any black American child have to attend an inferior school. Although many states fought the *Brown* decision, they eventually lost. The federal government, which had begun to take on more power during the Reconstruction era, won.

After the *Brown* ruling, Governor Frank Clement of Tennessee had called out the National Guard in Clinton, Tennessee, when race riots erupted. Governor Clement used the Guard to protect black children as they attended the newly integrated school. He confided to a few friends who were newspaper reporters that he believed the Supreme Court decision of *Brown* v. *Board of Education* was right. He vowed, "We are going to obey the law in this state."[27]

The *Brown* decision gave civil rights activists what they needed—the United States Constitution on their side. Encouraged, they continued their bold crusade for equal rights, and they had success. On June 19, 1963, President John Kennedy submitted his civil rights bill to Congress. The bill outlawed segregation in interstate public accommodations, allowed the Justice Department to force school integration, and cut off funds to federally funded programs that practiced discrimination. Congress eventually passed the civil rights bill. It became the historic Civil Rights Act of 1964.

What the Future Holds

In his speech on August 28, 1963, black civil rights leader Dr. Martin Luther King, Jr., told a crowd of thousands in Washington, D.C., about his dream for the future. King and other civil rights activists had organized the March on Washington for Jobs and Freedom. The crowd had gathered peacefully. Some two hundred fifty thousand people, black and white, listened as King stood

Dr. Martin Luther King, Jr., organized this March on Washington for Jobs and Freedom in 1963, where thousands gathered peacefully to demonstrate for civil rights.

Martin Luther King, Jr., became one of the most influential and well-respected black civil rights leaders of the twentieth century. His dream of peace and equality for all Americans inspired many to work toward improved race relations.

in the shadow of the statue of Abraham Lincoln at the Lincoln Memorial and spoke out passionately:

> I have a dream that my four children will one day live in a nation where they will not be judged by the color of their skin but by the content of their character.
> I have a dream today.
> I have a dream that one day . . . little black boys and black girls will be able to join hands with little white boys and white girls and walk together as sisters and brothers.
> I have a dream today.[28]

Can Dr. Martin Luther King's dream, which began with the hopes of the former slaves and the efforts of the Reconstructionists, come true? Much work still needs to be done. It depends on the participation of all Americans. In the words of United States President Bill Clinton, regarding his program called the President's Initiative on Race: "Building one America is our most important mission . . . money cannot buy it. Power cannot compel it. Technology cannot create it. It can only come from the human spirit."[29]

★ TIMELINE ★

1850—Fugitive Slave Law passed.

1857—*March 5*: *Dred Scott* decision announced by United States Supreme Court.

1860—*November 6*: Abraham Lincoln elected sixteenth president of the United States.

December 20: South Carolina secedes from the Union.

1861—*February 18*: Jefferson Davis sworn in as president of the Confederacy.

April 12: South Carolina fires on Fort Sumter; Civil War begins.

1863—*January 1*: Lincoln issues the Emancipation Proclamation.

December 8: Lincoln announces his Proclamation of Amnesty.

1864—*November 8*: Lincoln wins presidential election.

1865—*January 16*: General William Tecumseh Sherman issues Special Field Order No. 15.

April 9: Confederate General Robert E. Lee surrenders at Appomattox Court House.

April 15: Abraham Lincoln assassinated; Andrew Johnson becomes president.

May 29: President Johnson announces his plan for Reconstruction.

December 18: Thirteenth Amendment ratified.

1866—*April 9*: Civil Rights Act passed.

July 16: Freedmen's Bureau Act passed.

1867—*March*: Congress passes First Reconstruction Act; South divided into five military districts.

November: Blacks in the South vote for first time.

1868—Fourteenth Amendment ratified.

February 21: Andrew Johnson dismisses Secretary of War Edwin Stanton.

February 24: House of Representatives impeaches Andrew Johnson.

May 16: Andrew Johnson acquitted in Senate trial.

June 22–25: Alabama, Arkansas, Florida, Georgia, Louisiana, North Carolina, and South Carolina readmitted to the Union.

November 3: Freedmen vote in national election for first time; Ulysses S. Grant elected president.

1870—Virginia, Mississippi, and Texas readmitted to the Union.

March 30: Fifteenth Amendment ratified.

May 31: Congress passes Enforcement Act to protect black voters.

1871—*April 20*: Congress passes Ku Klux Act.

1872—*November 5*: Grant reelected.

1875—*March 1*: Congress passes Civil Rights Act.

1877—*March 2*: Rutherford Hayes elected president.

April: Hayes removes federal troops from South; Radical Reconstruction comes to an end.

1896—*May 18*: *Plessy* v. *Ferguson* establishes legal acceptability of "separate but equal" facilities.

1954—*May 17*: In *Brown* v. *Board of Education*, Supreme Court rejects *Plessy* v. *Ferguson*.

1964—*June 25*: Civil Rights Act passed.

★ CHAPTER NOTES ★

Chapter 1. The South in Ruins

1. Pauli Murray, *Proud Shoes: The Story of an American Family* (New York: Harper & Row, 1987), p. 170.

2. Ibid., pp. 170, 171.

3. Geoffrey C. Ward, *The Civil War, An Illustrated History*, with Ken Burns and Ric Burns (New York: Knopf, 1990), p. 9.

Chapter 2. War!

1. Geoffrey C. Ward, *The Civil War, An Illustrated History*, with Ken Burns and Ric Burns (New York: Knopf, 1990), pp. 377–381.

2. James M. McPherson, *What They Fought for, 1861–1865* (Baton Rouge: Louisiana State University Press, 1994), p. 42.

3. James M. McPherson, *Ordeal by Fire* (New York: Alfred A. Knopf, Inc., 1982), p. 35.

4. Peter Kolchin, *American Slavery, 1619–1877* (New York: Hill and Wang, 1993), pp. 111, 112.

5. Leon F. Litwack, *Been in the Storm So Long: The Aftermath of Slavery* (New York: Random House, Inc., 1980), p. 16.

6. Ibid., p. 17.

7. Ibid., p. 18.

8. Ibid., pp. 19, 23.

9. Charles L. Blockson, "Escape from Slavery, The Underground Railroad," *National Geographic*, vol. 166, no. 1, July 1984, p. 3.

10. John A. Garraty, *1,001 Things Everyone Should Know About American History* (New York: Doubleday, 1989), p. 6.

11. Kolchin, p. 181.

12. Edwin C. Rozwenc, ed., *Slavery as a Cause of the Civil War* (Boston: D.C. Heath & Company, 1963), p. 47.

13. James M. McPherson, *Battle Cry of Freedom: The Civil War Era* (New York: Oxford University Press, 1988), p. 244.

14. McPherson, *What They Fought For*, p. 10.

15. Ibid.

16. Ibid.

17. Ibid., p. 46.

18. Pauli Murray, *Proud Shoes: The Story of an American Family* (New York: Harper & Row, 1987), p. 149.

19. Ibid., p. 135.

20. Ibid., p. 155.

21. McPherson, *Ordeal by Fire*, p. 361.

22. Ibid.

Chapter 3. A Rough Start

1. Kenneth C. Davis, *Don't Know Much About the Civil War* (New York: Avon Books, 1997), p. 123.

2. Ibid., p. 161.

3. Eric Foner, *Reconstruction: America's Unfinished Revolution 1863–1877*, Perennial Library ed., ed. Henry Steele Commager and Richard B. Morris (New York: Harper & Row, 1988), p. 35.

4. Kenneth Stampp, *Era of Reconstruction 1865–1877* (New York: Alfred A. Knopf and Random House, Inc., 1965), p. 244.

5. In Jerome B. Agel, *Words That Make America Great* (New York: Random House, 1997), p. 214.

6. Douglas T. Miller, *Frederick Douglass & the Fight for Freedom* (New York: Facts on File Publications, 1988), p. 101.

7. Peter Kolchin, *American Slavery, 1619–1877* (New York: Hill and Wang, 1993), p. 208.

8. Foner, p. 35.

9. Kolchin, pp. 206–207.

10. Foner, p. 36.

11. James M. McPherson, *The Struggle for Equality* (Princeton, N.J.: Princeton University Press, 1964), p. 241.

12. In Geoffrey R. Stone, et al., *Constitutional Law* (Boston: Little, Brown and Company, 1991), p. lii.

13. James M. McPherson, *Battle Cry of Freedom: The Civil War Era* (New York: Oxford University Press, 1988), p. 150.

14. Kolchin, pp. 16, 17.

15. James M. McPherson, *Ordeal by Fire* (New York: Alfred A. Knopf, Inc., 1982), p. 94.

16. Foner, p. 176.

17. Ibid., p. 178.

18. Ibid., p. 180.

19. Miller, p. 113.

Chapter 4. Free at Last?

1. Eric Foner, *Reconstruction: America's Unfinished Revolution*, Perennial ed., ed. Henry Steele Commager and Richard B. Morris (New York: Harper & Row, 1988), p. 77.

2. Ibid., p. 80.

3. Ibid., p. 81.

4. Peter Kolchin, *American Slavery, 1619–1877* (New York: Hill and Wang, 1993), p. 127.

5. Leon F. Litwack, *Been in the Storm So Long: The Aftermath of Slavery* (New York: Random House, Inc., 1980), p. 305.

6. Foner, p. 82.

7. Litwack, p. 337.

8. Ibid., p. 449.

9. Pauli Murray, *Proud Shoes: The Story of an American Family* (New York: Harper & Row, 1987), pp. 170, 176, 179.

10. Foner, pp. 70, 71.

11. Litwack, pp. 400, 401.

12. Ibid., pp. 448, 449.

13. Fox Butterfield, *All God's Children, The Bosket Family and the American Tradition of Violence* (New York: Avon Books, 1995), p. 37.

Chapter 5. Johnson and the Radicals

1. Kenneth M. Stampp, *The Era of Reconstruction 1865–1877* (New York: Alfred A. Knopf and Random House, Inc., 1965), p. 51.

2. Ibid., p. 52.

3. Ibid., p. 55.

4. Ibid., pp. 60, 61.

5. Ibid., p. 59.

6. Eric Foner, *Reconstruction: America's Unfinished Revolution 1863–1877*, Perennial ed., ed. Henry Steele Commager and Richard B. Morris (New York: Harper & Row, 1988), p. 44.

7. Ibid.

8. Stampp, pp. 70, 71.

9. Foner, p. 191.

10. Stampp, pp. 71, 72.

11. Foner, p. 218.

12. Ibid.

13. W. E. Burghardt Du Bois, *Black Reconstruction in America* (New York: Russell & Russell, 1935, 1963), pp. 247, 256.

14. Lerone Bennett, Jr., *Black Power U.S.A. the Human Side of Reconstruction, 1865–1877*, ed. Brenda Biram (Chicago: Johnson Publishing Co., Inc., 1967), pp. 44, 45.

15. Ibid., p. 45.

16. James M. McPherson, *Ordeal by Fire* (New York: Alfred A. Knopf, Inc., 1982), p. 498.

17. Ibid., p. 500.

18. Peter Kolchin, *American Slavery, 1619–1877* (New York: Hill and Wang, 1993), pp. 209, 210.

19. Foner, pp. 199, 200.

20. McPherson, p. 512.

21. Foner, p. 251.

22. Bennett, p. 52.

23. Foner, p. 263.

24. Richard Hofstadter and Beatrice K. Hofstadter, eds., *Great Issues in American History: From Reconstruction to the Present Day, 1864–1981* (New York: Vintage Books, 1982), pp. 28–29.

25. Foner, p. 264.

26. Noel B. Gerson, *The Trial of Andrew Johnson* (Nashville and New York: Thomas Nelson, Inc., 1977), p. 76.

27. Foner, p. 265.

Chapter 6. The Ku Klux Klan

1. Lerone Bennett, Jr., *Black Power U.S.A. the Human Side of Reconstruction 1865–1877*, ed. Brenda Biram (Chicago: Johnson Publishing Co., Inc., 1967), p. 328.

2. Ibid.

3. Allen W. Trelease, *White Terror, The Ku Klux Klan Conspiracy and Southern Reconstruction*, ed. Kenneth B. Clark (New York: Harper & Row, 1971), p. 3.

4. Ibid., p. 4.

5. Ibid., p. 5.

6. Ibid., p. 9.

7. James P. Shenton, ed., *The Reconstruction, A Documentary History of the South After the War, 1865–1877* (New York: G. P. Putnam's Sons, 1963), p. 312.

8. Ibid., pp. 154, 155.

9. Eric Foner, *Reconstruction: America's Unfinished Revolution, 1863–1877*, Perennial ed., ed. Henry Steele Commager and Richard B. Morris (New York: Harper & Row, 1988), p. 426.

10. Trelease, p. 29.

11. Foner, p. 432.

12. Pauli Murray, *Proud Shoes: The Story of an American Family* (New York: Harper & Row, 1987), p. 221.

13. Foner, p. 433.

14. Ibid., p. 438.

15. Ibid., p. 437.

16. Ibid., p. 440.

17. Trelease, pp. 421, 422.

Chapter 7. The Radicals Take Charge

1. William Jay Jacobs, *Great Lives* (New York: Charles Scribner's Sons, 1990), p. 101.

2. W. E. Burghardt Du Bois, *Black Reconstruction in America*, 2nd ed. (New York: Russell & Russell, 1964), p. 342.

3. Richard W. Murphy and the editors of Time-Life Books, *The Civil War, The Nation Reunited, War's Aftermath* (Alexandria, Va.: Time-Life Books, Inc., 1987), p. 72.

4. Ibid.

5. Pauli Murray, *Proud Shoes: The Story of an American Family* (New York: Harper & Row, 1987), p. 197.

6. Murphy, p. 75.

7. Dorothy Levenson, *Reconstruction* (New York: Franklin Watts, Inc., 1987), pp. 44, 45.

8. Lerone Bennett, Jr., *Black Power U.S.A. the Human Side of Reconstruction, 1865–1877*, ed. Brenda Biram (Chicago: Johnson Publishing Co., Inc., 1967), p. 276.

9. John Hope Franklin, *Reconstruction After the Civil War* (Chicago: The University of Chicago Press, 1961), pp. 88, 89.

10. Bennett, p. 276.

11. Ibid., pp. 286, 287, 293.

12. Ibid., p. 285.

13. Emma Lou Thornbrough, *Black Reconstructionists* (Englewood Cliffs, N.J.: Prentice Hall, Inc., 1972), p. 6.

14. Ibid., p. 12.

15. Ibid., p. 138.

16. Eric Foner, *Reconstruction: America's Unfinished Revolution, 1863–1877*, Perennial ed., ed. Henry Steele Commager and Richard B. Morris (New York: Harper & Row, 1988), p. 294.

17. Franklin, p. 93.

18. James M. McPherson, *Ordeal by Fire* (New York: Alfred A. Knopf, Inc., 1982), p. 557.

19. Foner, p. 297.

20. Jeffrey D. Wert, *General James Longstreet* (New York: Simon & Schuster, 1993), pp. 410, 411.

21. In David Colbert, ed., *Eyewitness to America: 500 Years of America in the Words of Those Who Saw It Happen* (New York: Pantheon Books, 1997), p. 250.

22. Wert, p. 413.

23. Foner, p. 307.

Chapter 8. The South in Crisis

1. Pauli Murray, *Proud Shoes: The Story of an American Family* (New York: Harper & Row, 1987), p. 209.

2. Ibid.

3. Richard W. Murphy and the editors of Time-Life Books, *The Civil War, The Nation Reunited, War's Aftermath* (Alexandria, Va.: Time-Life Books, 1987), p. 76.

4. James M. McPherson, *Ordeal by Fire* (New York: Alfred A. Knopf, Inc., 1982), pp. 543, 544.

5. Ibid., p. 553.

6. Ibid.

7. Ibid., p. 544.

8. James M. McPherson, *The Struggle for Equality* (Princeton: Princeton University Press, 1964), p. 432.

9. Geoffrey R. Stone, et al., *Constitutional Law* (Boston: Little, Brown and Company, 1991), pp. lii–liii.

10. Kenneth M. Stampp, *Era of Reconstruction, 1865–1877* (New York: Alfred A. Knopf and Random House, Inc., 1965), p. 207.

11. Murphy, p. 88.

12. Ibid.

13. Ibid., p. 97.

14. Ibid., p. 98.

15. Allen W. Trelease, *White Terror, The Ku Klux Klan Conspiracy and Southern Reconstruction*, ed. Kenneth B. Clark (New York: Harper & Row, 1971), p. 404.

16. Ibid., p. 415.

17. Eric Foner, *Reconstruction: America's Unfinished Revolution, 1863–1877*, Perennial ed., ed. Henry Steele Commager and Richard B. Morris (New York: Harper & Row, 1988), p. 468.

18. McPherson, *Ordeal by Fire*, p. 567.

19. Foner, p. 500.

20. Murphy, p. 111.

21. McPherson, *Ordeal by Fire*, p. 570.

22. Murphy, p. 112.

23. McPherson, *Ordeal by Fire*, p. 571.

24. Murphy, pp. 125–127.

Chapter 9. Legacy

1. Peter Kolchin, *American Slavery, 1619–1877* (New York: Hill and Wang, 1993), p. 234.

2. Eric Foner, *Reconstruction: America's Unfinished Revolution, 1863–1877*, Perennial ed., ed. Henry Steele Commager and Richard B. Morris (New York: Harper & Row, 1988), p. 567.

3. Dorothy Levenson, *Reconstruction* (New York: Franklin Watts, Inc., 1987), p. 60.

4. Foner, p. 576.

5. Ibid., p. 581.

6. Ibid., p. 582.

7. Kolchin, p. 148.

8. Catherine Clinton, *Tara Revisited: Women, War, and the Plantation Legend*, ed. Constance Herndon (New York: Abbeville Publishing Group, 1995), p. 195.

9. Ibid., p. 201.

10. Leon F. Litwack, *Trouble in Mind: Black Southerners in the Age of Jim Crow* (New York: Alfred A. Knopf, 1998), p. xiv.

11. Ibid., p. 232.

12. Personal interview with Timothy Tyrone Taylor, October 20, 1998.

13. Litwack, p. 64.

14. John A. Garraty, *1,001 Things Everyone Should Know About American History* (New York: Doubleday, 1989), p. 34.

15. Litwack, p. 243.

16. Pauli Murray, *Proud Shoes: The Story of an American Family* (New York: Harper & Row, 1987), p. 269.

17. Litwack, p. 13.

18. Litwack, pp. 284–285.

19. Ibid., p. 286.

20. Ibid., p. 289.

21. Ibid., p. 288.

22. Ibid., p. 289.

23. Ibid., p. 297.

24. Clinton, p. 209.

25. Ibid., p. 212.

26. Lisa Cozzens, *Early Civil Rights Struggles*, 1995, <http://www.watson.org>, pp. 1, 2.

27. David Halberstam, *The Children* (New York: Random House, 1998), p. 11.

28. Jerome B. Agel, ed., *Words That Make America Great* (New York: Random House, 1997), p. 166.

29. President William Jefferson Clinton, *The President's Initiative on Race* brochure, June 14, 1997.

★ FURTHER READING ★

Books

Foner, Eric. *Reconstruction: America's Unfinished Revolution, 1863–1877*, ed. Henry Steele Commager and Richard B. Morris. New York: Harper & Row, 1988.

Kent, Zachary. *The Civil War: "A House Divided."* Hillside, N.J.: Enslow Publishers, Inc., 1994.

Levenson, Dorothy. *Reconstruction*. New York: Franklin Watts, Inc., 1987.

Litwack, Leon F. *Trouble in Mind: Black Southerners in the Age of Jim Crow*. New York: Alfred A. Knopf, 1998.

Sawyer, Kem Knapp. *The Underground Railroad in American History*. Springfield, N.J.: Enslow Publishers, Inc., 1997.

Internet Addresses

American Civil War Home Page. February 24, 1995. <http://sunsite.utk.edu/civil-war/warweb.html> (May 7, 1999).

Library of Congress. *American Memory*. n.d. <http://lcweb2.loc.gov/ammem> (May 7, 1999).

"Opposing Views on Reconstruction." *An Outline of American History*. 1997. <http://odur.let.rug.nl/~usa/H/1990/ch5_p11.htm> (May 7, 1999).

★ INDEX ★